GHOST STORIES
of California

D0956540

BARBARA SMITH

LONE
PINE

The Publisher: Lone Pine Publishing

87 East Pender Street
Vancouver, BC V6A 1S9
Canada

1808 B Street NW, Suite 140
Auburn, WA 98001
USA

Website: www.lonepinepublishing.com

Canadian Cataloguing in Publication Data

Smith, Barbara, 1947 –
    Ghost stories of California

    ISBN 13: 978-1-55105-237-3
    ISBN 10: 1-55105-237-7

    1. Ghosts—California. 2. Legends—California. I. Title.
GR580.S65 2000   398.2'0979405   C00-910350-3

Editorial Director: Nancy Foulds
Project Editor: Randy Williams
Production Manager: Jody Reekie
Book Design: Monica Triska
Layout & Production: Arlana Anderson-Hale

Photos Courtesy of: The Winchester Mystery House® (p. 19, 20), Karen Knight (p. 25), General Services Administration File, National Archives, San Bruno (p. 44), Dolores Steele (p. 66, 67, 68, 71, 73, 74, 76, 80, 81, 83), Kristin Johnson (p. 90), Robert Smith (p. 100, 106, 175), Jan Jones (p. 112), The Hotel del Coronado (p. 118, 119), Harry Fechtman for the Hotel del Coronado (p. 124, 125), The Hollywood Roosevelt Hotel (p. 129, 137), Barbara Smith (p. 149, 158), The Great American Melodrama & Vaudeville (p. 198), Conejo Players Theatre (p. 204), and The Woodland Opera House (p. 207).

We acknowledge the financial support of the Government of Canada through the Canada Book Fund (CBF) for our publishing activities.

 Canadian   Patrimoine
Heritage   canadien

PC: P33

Dedication

This book is dedicated to Grant Kennedy, Shane Kennedy and the entire staff at Lone Pine Publishing. Thank you, one and all.

For my grandsons and their peers—who will need forests as much as books—arrangements have been made to plant trees to compensate for the paper used in printing this volume.

Contents

Acknowledgements

Because this was to be my eighth book in a series of true ghost stories, I expected that I would be able to stay on top of the project at all times. Much to my delight, I found I couldn't! The people I contacted in California were so knowledgeable and helpful that, time after time, I came away from one interview with a lead on another great story. For this reason I would like to extend a warm thank you to everyone contacted during the research phase of writing this book. To all the folks mentioned in the stories, many thanks for your friendly support. Your time and trouble were much appreciated. Some people, for understandable reasons, asked to remain anonymous. You, of course, will not be named— but you, too, are sincerely thanked.

In addition, I was helped immensely by the generosity and kindness of the following individuals: Paranormal researcher extraordinaire, W. Ritchie Benedict of Calgary, Alberta; Ritchie's talents and generosity are amazing. Fellow author (and dear friend) Jo-Anne Christensen of Edmonton, Alberta, generously shared both resources and ideas with me. Andy Honigman of *Fate Magazine* quickly and graciously supplied me with an obscure article that I needed. Kristin Johnson, author of *Unfortunate Emigrants*, shared her expertise about the Donner Party. Thank you for also sharing the illustration, Kristin—your faith and trust were heartwarming. Karen Knight of Sherwood Park, Alberta, kept my project in mind while visiting San Diego and brought me back a photograph of the Whaley House. Once again, Dr. Barrie Robinson of Edmonton improved my work by tactfully and patiently reviewing my stories. Thank you, Barrie. My husband, Bob Smith, attended to many supportive (and often thankless!) chores for me. Many of the photographs in this book were taken by Dolores Steele, a talented and generous Californian. I shall miss your cheery e-mail messages, Dolores.

The Public Relations staffs of the Hotel del Coronado and the Winchester Mystery House® were efficient and very helpful. Loanne Wullaert of the Ventura Theatre referred me to Nathan Beavers and Dustin Wagner, both of whom generously shared their experiences with me during lengthy telephone interviews. Nadine Salotines, the unofficial historian of Woodland Opera House, told me about their ghost and then mailed extensive background material my way. Dick Johnson and Jean Murray of the Conejo Playhouse were also very helpful, as were Linda Bredemann of the Moorpark Melodrama Theater, Marianne Boos of the Hollywood Roosevelt Hotel, Jeff Kean of the Woodland Opera House, and Evelyn Shirbroun, owner of the Joshua Tree Inn. Thanks are also due to Dana Andersen of Edmonton, Alberta and Scott Armstrong of Sacramento for the time committed to our interview.

I owe a further debt of gratitude to the many talented paranormal investigators who have gone before. These people, who are often local experts, have done an invaluable job of researching possible explanations for particular hauntings. As a storyteller and folklore collector, my experience has been significantly enriched by their groundbreaking efforts.

My efforts, and those of the people named above, would have been made in vain without the support I received from the talented people who make up the staff at Lone Pine Publishing. Working with all of you is a pleasure. Special thanks to Nancy Foulds, Patrizia Sorgiovanni and Randy Williams.

Introduction

Without a doubt, California is one of the most geographically spectacular and diverse locations on the face of this planet. And its history is at least as compelling as its geography. From the desert to the ocean, from the Gold Rush to Silicon Valley, the nearly 156,000 square miles within California's boundaries are unlike any other place on earth.

In researching this collection of ghost stories I found, time and time again, that much of California's history has been shaped by its geography. This history has created a rich cache of unique, local legends—California folklore—and much of that lore includes ghosts. In addition, there are more recent ghost stories—not to mention the hauntings that are currently occurring!

Having said that, I may have inadvertently implied that I have an iron-clad definition for both "ghost" and "haunting." If so, I must correct that impression. Although I've been collecting ghost stories for more than 10 years, all I can claim is to have developed some firm theories as to what a ghost is *not*. A ghost is not a cute, white cartoon character, nor is it a human figure draped with a white sheet. A ghost is also not necessarily a filmy, gauzy apparition, although some certainly fit that description.

Frederic Myers, one of the founding members of the old and honorable Society for Psychical Research in England, suggested in his book, *Human Personality and Its Survival of Bodily Death* (1903), that ghosts are unaware of themselves and incapable of thought. With all due respect to the erudite Dr. Myers, I wonder whether that last statement is true for *all* hauntings. Some ghosts seem only to be continuing with their life's business, completely oblivious to the world of the living that surrounds them, while others have specific tasks—such as delivering a message from beyond the grave—that they are determined to perform.

To add to the confusion, an issue of semantics arises. Most would agree that there are few true synonyms in the English language. Nonetheless, I have chosen to use the following words interchangeably; specter, spirit, shade, entity, presence, revenant, manifestation, phantom, wraith and, of course, ghost. While I've never found an exact definition for what a ghost is, the phenomenon *does* exist in all cultures and has been noted throughout history.

Not all ghosts present themselves visually in the shape of humans. Those that do are more properly called apparitions. Just because a ghost is not seen (i.e., is not an apparition) does not mean that there isn't a spirit in the vicinity. The specter may manifest itself only in the form of a sensation—that feeling that you are not alone even though no one else is physically present. Ghosts can also manifest as odors—both pleasant and unpleasant. Other evidence of a paranormal occurrence can include ghostly lights and even phantom sounds.

A poltergeist is a rare type of supernatural being that can be identified by its noisy and even violent behaviors. It will often move objects and can actually wreak havoc on its surrounding environment. Poltergeists are always associated with people, rather than places. They have been known to follow certain people for years, through a succession of moves from one residence to another—and even from one continent to another.

Retrocognition, which has been described as seeing or in some other manner *sensing* the past, is an especially fascinating type of ghostly phenomenon. Some students of the paranormal believe that most, if not all, hauntings can be attributed to retrocognition. Retrocognition is defined as a temporary displacement in time; this dislocation allows the person affected an opportunity to review or experience historical events. In other words, the energy once created is somehow detected and replayed in a manner that can be likened to either an audio- or videotape on a continuous loop. The psychic energy exuded has become anchored in the atmosphere. Acceptance of this theory implies a "place memory"— the concept that certain events are embedded in a given place and continue to resonate. These are also called "residual hauntings."

It has been suggested that retrocognition (also known as post-cognition) actually occurs much more frequently than is commonly recognized, but that the fleeting temporal displacement is simply written off as the witness's imagination. If this is so, then perhaps we should be paying closer attention to momentary shifts in our perception when we experience them.

The opposite of retrocognition is precognition—seeing or sensing an event that has not yet occurred. When such an experience is accompanied by a presence or ghost, the presence is called a "forerunner."

One further type of phantom energy is the manifestation of ghost lights or ignes fatui. These luminous paranormal occurrences, which often occur in cemeteries, have fascinated countless people over the centuries.

But why do spectral phenomena exist? The theory of "leftover energy"—physical and emotional—is frequently used to explain the existence of ghosts. This theory is closely related to the concept of "psychic imprint"—the idea that the essence of a person or an event has somehow been "stamped" onto the environment in which that person lived or a traumatic or violent event took place. The deceased person's soul has effectively left an indelible mark on the physical world; in simple terms, he or she has become a ghost.

Some say that ghosts are simply beings who either don't know that the body they once occupied is now deceased or, for some reason, can't accept that death.

Because some people are so much more likely than others to be aware of a ghost's presence, it is possible that spirits are all around us but are detectable only by our (nearly atrophied) sixth sense. Rather than perceiving otherworldly sensations with our familiar five senses, we may only notice the hair on our arms or on the back of our necks standing on end, or become aware of a generalized tingling sensation in our skin. And what of that disconcerting feeling that we are not alone—that we are being watched, even though our five senses fail to confirm the existence of any other presence nearby? Scientists have suggested that humans do indeed possess a rarely used sixth sense, located in the vomeronasal organ (in the nose), that is capable of detecting pheromones—chemicals released into the air in minute quantities by many species as a way of communicating with others of their kind.

Perhaps the vomeronasal organ also detects or senses energies exuded from disembodied spirits but, because we are not used to consciously responding to messages from this sense, we are unable to recognize the messages as anything more than a vague feeling that "something" is close to us. It is quite possible that some humans are more sensitive to such subtleties than others. Children, for example, seem to be more sensitive to otherworldly presences than adults. Over time most adults have come to rely almost exclusively on their other five senses and therefore ignore—or fail to respond to—sensations picked up by their sixth sense.

Those adults who *do* seem to recognize and act upon messages from their sixth sense are usually referred to as "psychics" or "sensitives." Though this sensitivity is likely inborn, it can apparently be enhanced with practice—or diminished through neglect. Perhaps the variations in sensitivity from person to person explain why some people are more likely than others to encounter a ghost.

Behind all of these suppositions lurks a further unknown: Does a ghostly encounter originate with the living person who is experiencing the encounter, or with the ghost itself? The answer is debatable but, because many people have reported seeing or sensing the same spirit either at the same or different times, the entities and events chronicled in this book are unlikely to be mere figments of the observers' imaginations. Just as there is an invisible energy that exists between magnets and metal, there is growing evidence that people generate the same kind of magnetic energy—and that this energy remains in the environment even after death. Like the relationship between the metal and the magnet, you can neither see nor touch this energy, but you know it's there.

Some forms of this ghostly energy are incredibly tenacious. For example, the ghosts of Roman soldiers are still occasionally spotted roaming the English countryside where they battled centuries ago, but few ghosts are that ancient. Because I've never heard or read of any place or person being haunted by the ghost of a prehistoric cave dweller, I presume that, like all forms of energy, ghosts eventually weaken and dissipate.

In the presence of a ghost or during an active haunting, witnesses will usually note predictable and distinguishable changes in their environment. Such changes often include a sudden, dramatic temperature drop that is localized, though it may encompass a large area. Drafts, odors or noises—all of which are apparently sourceless—may also be present.

The narratives in this book are reports of real events. We all know that life, as we live it, is anything but neat. As a result, these accounts tend to be a bit more ragged than the stories we are used to reading. A fictional tale of a haunting will be structured with a predictable presentation: a beginning, a middle and an end. The incidents recorded here refuse to be that orderly. Sometimes they are merely fragments, which can be somewhat frustrating in a world so fond of tidy resolutions. We tend to find it more satisfying when loose ends are bound up in the last sentence of a tale. Nonetheless, I hope you will find—as I have come to—that in the instances where there isn't enough information to tell a traditional story, the parts that are missing are every bit as provocative as the parts that remain.

This collection is not intended as an attempt to alter anyone's belief system with my personal convictions or explanations. My intent is to entertain and to possibly prompt thought in areas that you might not otherwise have considered exploring. Though I do not pretend to be an educator, if reading this book introduces you to facets of California's history or geography with which you were previously unfamiliar, then I will be delighted.

If you have any additions to the stories contained in this volume or personal experiences with the paranormal that you would like to share with the author, please contact me through Lone Pine Publishing. I'd love to hear from you. In the meantime, do enjoy this unique perspective on the beautiful State of California and its colorful folklore.

Chapter 1
HAUNTED HOUSES

*For most of us, our home
is an important part of our life.
Whether it's a single room in a
boarding house, a boat, a ranch,
a city bungalow or a condominium
apartment in a downtown high-rise,
we humans tend to develop strong
emotional attachments to our homes.
This intensity can help to promote
paranormal activity such as
a haunting. However, the following
stories give ample proof of other,
stranger means by which our homes
can become haunted.*

The Winchester Mystery House®

Leonard and Sarah Pardee belonged to the upper echelon of society in New Haven, Connecticut. They enjoyed all the advantages that money could buy, and when Sarah presented Leonard with a tiny, perfect baby daughter in 1840, the couple was sure their lives were complete. They named the new arrival after her mother and proceeded to lavish the child with all of the many benefits at their disposal.

Six years before little Sarah's birth, Oliver Winchester of New England had married Jane Ellen Hope. Although Oliver was by that time a wealthy man, he had been born into abject poverty and had never forgotten the hardships he had suffered because of it. All his life he worked to expand his financial empire and to ensure that his children were given advantages that he'd been denied as a boy.

William, the Winchester's only son, grew up during a period when his father's industrial interests shifted from carpentry to textiles and finally to the growth industry of the time—firearms. The guns may have seemed a contradiction to the intimate, cultured and elite society peopled by families like the Pardees and Winchesters, but much of the rest of the country consisted of settlers, cowboys and gold miners. Such folks were creating their own societies, societies not nearly so filled with niceties, order, laws and civilities. These were societies in which firearms were often the single determining factor between success and failure.

William Winchester's upbringing was, therefore, at least as privileged as Sarah Pardee's, who, by her teens, had been well-schooled in languages and music. To add to her good fortune,

Sarah was as pretty as she was petite. Not surprisingly, the girl was the belle of many balls. The most eligible bachelors of the day were crushed with disappointment when it was announced that William Winchester had won Sarah Pardee's hand in marriage.

The young couple's happiness was tragically short-lived. Their only child, a daughter born four years after their marriage, died of a mysterious ailment when she was just a few months old. Sarah's grief over the loss was virtually all-encompassing. She never became pregnant again.

In 1880, William's father died, leaving control of the Winchester corporate empire to his only son. Sadly, William himself died less than three months later. This left Sarah Pardee Winchester an incredibly wealthy, childless widow. It also left her completely devastated and utterly unable to cope.

To add to the woman's misery, her body had become riddled with painful arthritis. Friends tried to convince Sarah to move to a milder climate but she stubbornly maintained that she had no interest in doing so.

At this time, a fascination with spiritualism was sweeping the western world. Psychically sensitive mediums were in huge demand. Of course, many of these "psychics" were complete frauds, but research does indicate that there were then, as there are now, a few who were genuinely gifted. Adam Cooms, of Boston, was apparently one of those. When Sarah heard of Cooms's abilities, she traveled to consult with him. If that meeting had not taken place, it's safe to say that curious tourists in California would have one less place to visit—it was Cooms who advised Sarah Winchester to create the architectural edifice that we know today as the very haunted Winchester Mystery House®.

Sarah's session with Cooms was obviously a convincing one. The psychic knew nothing about William Winchester but nonetheless apparently summoned the spirit of Sarah's late husband to the meeting. Through Cooms, the ghost explained that the spirits of the tens of thousands killed by the rifle that bore his name were tormenting him—and that those same ghosts would also prevent Sarah from living in peace. In order to accommodate their ghostly demands, William advised Sarah that she would have to leave the east and travel until she came to an unnamed location. She would know the right place when she found it, he assured her. Once there, the distraught widow was to buy the property and begin constructing additions to the existing structure. The tormenting spirits apparently wanted her to house them and, because the Winchester rifle was continuing to kill people, additions would have to be built continuously to accommodate an increasingly large population of phantoms.

Determined to honor the wishes of her deceased husband, Sarah Winchester drew on her enormous wealth to travel west. She eventually purchased an eight-room house on a tract of land in San Jose. As soon as she had done so, she hired a crew of carpenters and instructed them to begin adding rooms to the place. They did, and the construction that began that day did not stop for the next 39 years.

As the weird mansion evolved, Sarah Winchester herself became increasingly strange. On the rare occasions that she went into town, she often chose and purchased fabric from which to have her dresses made. To ensure that no one else would have a dress of the same material, she always bought the entire bolt. As the months wore on, she became a recluse, shutting herself off from the outside world completely—even, it is said, declining to acknowledge a visit from President Theodore Roosevelt. Her entire existence was devoted to mollifying the spirits.

The continuous additions to her property were intended not only to house the ever-increasing number of souls who met death as a result of the rifle that bore the Winchester family name, but

Sarah continued to build additions to the mansion—to make more room for the many ghosts sharing her residence—for 39 years.

also to confuse any evil spirits. Toward this end, Sarah ordered the most peculiar configurations created in the building. She felt that secret passageways, miles of switchback corridors, doors which opened to blank walls, stairways that lead nowhere, and chimneys that stopped short of the roof line would all help to keep those malignant phantoms from finding and tormenting her.

Even with all of those precautions, the pitiful woman lived in a state of constant terror. She slept in a different bedroom every night in an apparently successful attempt to keep the possibly vengeful wraiths from finding her.

In addition to the never-ending construction, Sarah also sought to appease the spectral entities by entertaining them. She spent agonizing hours playing the piano and organ with her painfully arthritic fingers so that the spirits could enjoy dancing to the music she made. These dance sessions often followed elaborate "dinner parties" at which phantoms were not just the guests of honor but the *only* guests. As the sole living person in the dining

Disturbed young widow Sarah Winchester hosted elaborate dinner parties for the dead in this beautiful but bizarre mansion.

room, Sarah would preside at the head of a beautifully set table and order her servants to serve lavish five-course meals to her ghostly guests.

These invisible guests always numbered an even dozen because Sarah was convinced that there was magic in the number 13 and, in this way, she would always be the 13th at the table. Her obsession with 13 ruled more than just her mealtime entertaining. Staircases each had to have 13 steps; rooms, 13 windows; windows, 13 panes; chandeliers, 13 lights. The house even had 13 bathrooms.

While all of this is intriguing and undeniably bizarre, is it safe, or even reasonable, to presume that Sarah Winchester was truly haunted by the spirits of those killed with the Winchester rifle? Or was the woman merely insane? History has assured that the answers to these questions are not straightforward. There's no point in denying that Sarah had little connection with reality by the time she settled in California. Since her death in 1922, however, many people have determined that her strange architectural legacy really is home to ghosts—even to the ghost of Sarah herself!

Because there is little else such an odd building could be used for, Winchester House has been a popular tourist attraction since the year after the haunted widow's death. Thousands of people are guided through the house every year and, even with the majority of rooms sealed off, visitors are in the enormous, rambling structure for more than an hour. Some of those visitors have testified to seeing, hearing, or feeling unearthly spirits. The staff, who are obviously considerably more accustomed to the atmosphere of the house, have also reported encounters with spirits. When psychics have been brought in, their insights have confirmed the presence of ghosts.

Sylvia Brown, a respected California-based psychic, spent a night in the house with a few of her fellow paranormal researchers. She claimed to have heard organ music, which she presumed to be ghostly echoes of the concerts Sarah so painfully performed for the spirits. Oddly, Brown's colleagues heard nothing. For this reason, it might have been easy to dismiss Brown's findings—except that the tape recorder, which had been running throughout their stay in the house, recorded exactly what Sylvia Brown had heard. In addition, all those present that night detected inexplicable cold spots in areas where no drafts would have been possible. They also watched in fascination as ghost lights appeared, moved about, and then vanished into different parts of the house.

Another psychic, Warren Capling, had a similar experience. He too listened to phantom organ music, but, interestingly, he was in the bedroom where Sarah Winchester died when he was treated to the impromptu concert—and there has never been an organ in that area of the house. Immediately after the music stopped, a ghost light traveled across the bedroom, stopping for a moment at the bed before vanishing.

On Halloween in 1975, psychics Jeanne Borgen and Joy Adams spent an unnerving time in Winchester House. Borgen watched in horror as Adams's body was taken over by a spirit—probably the spirit of Sarah Winchester herself. Sarah has also appeared as a silent apparition in various rooms and passageways and has even been seen outside on the beautiful grounds that surround the house.

Sue Sale, an employee of the haunted house, was shocked to see Sarah's image sitting at the kitchen table. The manifestation was so lifelike that Sale initially assumed it was an actor dressed for the part. Others who've encountered the former owner's presence agree that it is a strong spirit, but also use words such as "gentle" and "kind" when describing what they've seen.

Other employees hear the sounds of someone breathing and of whispering voices but can never track down their source. Doors often mysteriously slam shut in unoccupied parts of the building.

Tourists who take photographs while in the house are frequently treated to an extra image in a few of the frames. Ghost lights are etched on the film of some negatives, even though the photographer saw nothing like them when he or she was setting up or taking the shot. One amazing picture reveals the form of a man dressed in overalls, although no one present saw his image at the time.

At least a few of the ghosts inhabiting Winchester House seem to enjoy practical jokes. They not only unlock secure doors, but once, after employee Allen Weitzel had finished turning off all the lights in the house, locking it up, and going out toward his car, he looked back at the house to make sure that he hadn't missed the lights in any of the rooms. Content that the house was in darkness, he made his way to his car. From there, he looked back again. This time, all of the third floor windows were brightly lit up.

Weitzel was also the butt of what was possibly a ghostly prank. He came to work one day to find everything in his office wet. The water didn't leak in through natural means because the walls, ceiling and floor were bone dry.

One employee, then-Director of Operations Roger LaFountain, actually hoped to find water seepage in an electrical fixture; he thought that water might explain why a light bulb had exploded. Unfortunately for his peace of mind, he found that both the socket and the area around it were completely dry. Although it is highly unusual for a light bulb to explode spontaneously, it is technically possible. Given that the event occurred in the very haunted Winchester House, though, it is equally likely that the "accident" was caused by some paranormal means.

Even with the evidence cited above, we cannot know for sure whether Sarah Winchester was, in fact, haunted by the ghosts of the souls killed by the Winchester Repeating Rifle. It is certainly reasonable, however, to assume that the Winchester Mystery House is now thoroughly haunted—if not by the rifle's victims, then certainly by Sarah and some of her exceptionally loyal staff. Best of all, this haunted venue is open to the public and the administration is very accepting of the fact that the house is home to ghosts.

The Whaley House

The Whaley House in Old Town, San Diego, is the oldest brick structure still standing in Southern California. And, it is haunted—so haunted that the site is acknowledged by the United States Department of Commerce as "one of 30 ghost houses" in the country.

Thomas Whaley began construction of his family's home in the spring of 1856. Thankfully, a group of concerned citizens saved his efforts from certain demolition 100 years later and the Whaley House is now a museum. Because it's open to the public and officially recognized as being haunted, Whaley House is a splendid spot for ghost hunters to visit. While the sheer number of spirits occupying the house is astounding, the diversity of their ghostly activities and the longevity of the hauntings themselves are also most impressive.

The house was occupied by members of the family until Corrine Lillian Whaley, Thomas and Anna's youngest daughter, died at the age of 89 in 1953. The last years of the woman's life were spent cloistered on the main floor of the two-story home. While sorting through Lillian's belongings after her death, friends discovered a notation she had made explaining that she felt "at least one of the ghosts" didn't want her presence on the second story of the house.

This may well have been the spirit of "Yankee" Jim Robinson, who has been haunting the property since he was hanged on the tract of land where the Whaley House would be built five years later. It is hardly surprising that Robinson's spirit is somewhat restless, because his crime was not one that usually resulted in a death sentence. He and two other men were charged with theft. His accomplices were sentenced to jail terms but, for undocumented

The historic Whaley House, in San Diego's Old Town, is home to a large number of very active supernatural entities, making it a splendid spot for ghost hunters to visit.

reasons, it was decided that Yankee Jim should be hanged. The gallows were erected on the exact spot where Thomas Whaley would later build his house.

In addition to the brutality of Yankee Jim's sentence, it seems that the structure prepared for his hanging was poorly constructed. As a result, his death was not the quick and painless one that it should have been. Rather than dying instantly of a broken neck, Robinson expired slowly and painfully of asphyxiation. Perhaps this is why the criminal's spirit has never gone on to its eternal rest.

Jim's footsteps are still heard walking across the floor of the upper story of Whaley House. He routinely makes his way from the upstairs sitting room to the top of the staircase. His manifestation is also occasionally seen in the doorway between the parlor and the reading room—dangling from his executioner's rope. Witnesses agree that it is not a pretty sight.

Robinson may have been the first of the property's ghostly inhabitants, but he now shares his eternity with a collection of entities. It has been suggested that, because the house is close to a cemetery and already haunted, it has become something of a meeting place for spirits. The ghosts who congregate in the house are so plentiful and so vibrant that photographers have managed to capture a few of their images.

In addition to Yankee Jim, other ghosts who are recognized include most of the members of the Whaley family. It would appear that their images have returned to their earthly home after death. A spirit described as being man with a mustache, wearing pantaloons, a frock coat and a wide-brimmed hat, is almost certainly Thomas Whaley himself. Usually his apparition is very solid and clearly visible but, once seen, vanishes in an instant. At other times, it's seen as an indistinct blur at the entrance to what used to be his office. Although the ghost's face is not recognizable when it appears in that form, his actions are familiar; moments after the phantom is seen, invisible papers are heard being shuffled in Thomas's otherwise empty office. Occasionally he is also seen walking the grounds of the property, and when a ghostly baritone laugh echoes through the house, it's presumed that Whaley is amused by something.

The female ghost most often seen may either be that of Thomas's wife Anna or perhaps their older daughter. Whoever she is, the lady's devotion to her family's well-being has continued after death. She stands in one of the bedrooms, apparently folding clothes that are invisible to all but herself. Whether this particular image is Anna or not, she is definitely still part of her house. She's been clearly seen on some occasions, but other times her presence is more subtle; the fragrance of perfume and phantom cooking odors are commonly credited to Anna, who was known to have enjoyed entertaining.

When Anna's ghost systematically makes her way throughout the rooms of her former residence carrying a candle, staff in the museum assumes that the former lady of the house is simply making her rounds before retiring for the night. In the mornings, the woman's spirit has been seen tending to her beloved flower garden. That's also where the ghost of Dolly Varden, the Whaley family's dog, is usually seen.

Music was an important component of Whaley family life, and it seems to have remained important after their death. Visitors to the house, as well those who work there, have heard a female voice singing a song ironically entitled "Home Again." Musical instruments such as the piano, organ, violin, mandolin—and even a music box—are also heard being played.

The ghostly echoes of a long-ago meeting continue to resonate so clearly in Whaley's study that an entire group of phantoms can be clearly seen. The images are of men, dressed appropriately for the 19th century, seemingly involved in a very serious conversation. The apparitions are so distinct that witnesses note pocket watches, hair color, eye color, and the different body sizes and shapes of the various participants in the ghostly gathering that has never been adjourned. Even when that vision is not apparent, cold spots and cool breezes are scattered around that room although there is no physical explanation for such phenomena.

The most poignant image in the Whaley House is that of seven-year-old Annabelle Washburn. The little girl died in the Whaley's kitchen, brought inside after she ran into a clothesline strung in the yard at precisely the height of the child's neck. Despite her tragic death, she's a happy and, of course, child-like spirit who simply runs throughout the house and the adjacent yard.

A female apparition wearing a green gingham dress who sits in one of the bedrooms and a dark-skinned woman wearing large gold hoop earrings have not yet been identified. Whether they were associated with the house in life or simply attracted there after death is unclear.

An annex to the Whaley House originally served as a court-room. Today, it has been refurbished to reflect how it would have looked during those days. Some of the trials must have been extremely emotion-laden, because it occasionally sounds as though court's still in session—even when the room is empty. Further-more, protective chains set up around the courtroom move up and down and in a swaying motion when no one is near them. The movements stop whenever a human being comes close by.

In other parts of the house, door knobs rattle, light fixtures swing and tinkle, kitchen utensils hanging from hooks on a wall move sideways as though they were pendulums, burglar alarms malfunction and windows mysteriously open. One visitor to the house watched in awe as a bedcover moved when he was near the bed. At other times, the clomping of unseen horses' hooves are still heard outside as though a phantom carriage were arriving at the house.

The ghostly sounds of a billiard game being played is a phe-nomenon that has been examined in depth. Sandy Stokes, a reporter with the *Riverside Press-Enterprise*, accepted renowned paranormal-researcher Richard Senate's advice to keep her tape recorder running the entire time she was in the house. Although she'd intended to tape her interview with the staff, she initially thought that his idea of the constantly running tape was a rather silly one. When Stokes's session in the house was over, however, she played the recording back and quickly changed her mind; the tape had distinctly picked up the sounds of a pool game being played.

These particular sounds were especially puzzling because no one had been playing pool in the house while Stokes had been there. As a matter of fact, when she checked with the administra-tion of the Whaley House, Stokes discovered that, although one of the rooms had once been set aside for billiards, no one had played such a game in the house since the 1920s.

Stokes and Senate took the tape recording to an expert in the field of recorded ghostly sounds (EVP or electronic voice phenomenon). The expert compared the sounds the reporter had captured with everything he could think of that might come close to replicating those on the tape. Nothing was exactly right, not even the sound of actual billiard balls being struck. Further investigation revealed that, because not all billiard balls are made of the same material, identical-looking balls can sound very different when struck.

When the journalist consulted Terry Moldenhauer, a collector of billiard memorabilia, he indicated that the best billiard balls in the late 1800s and early 1900s would have been made of ivory. Luckily, Moldenhauer owned a few of the antiques. When Sandy Stokes and Richard Senate recorded the sounds made by those ivory pieces striking one another and compared them to the sounds of the spectral pool game that Sandy had recorded, the sounds were found to be identical. It would seem Ms. Stokes had recorded the sounds of a game that had been played many years before.

Judging from all the activity that continues to resonate in the Whaley House, it would seem that the magnificent old home is an excellent haunting spot, not only for the spirits of the long-deceased but also for flesh and blood human beings who are curious about ghosts.

Presence on the Property

In the 1960s, real estate developers began to build tract housing around Santa Ana in an area known as Westminster. Of course, the first residents to move into those homes were certainly not the first people to ever live on that particular stretch of land. Local records verify that, in 1911, a tiny community called Bolsa—dependent on ranching and orange groves—was located there. At least one of the homes in this village had been built as early as 1871. Defying amazing odds, that house survived until the late 1950s, when it was finally torn down to begin building the contemporary development.

Bolsa hadn't just consisted of orange groves, ranches and houses. Like any community, the most important part of Bolsa was its citizens. Unfortunately, as the following story will bear out, the spirits of some of those long-ago inhabitants made life extremely difficult for at least two families who lived in the area during the 1960s.

The Trausch family, Carole and her husband (whom we'll call Jim) and their three daughters, Diane, Megan and Heather, moved into the Westminster tract in 1966. They were the second tenants in their particular unit, which had two bedrooms just up a flight of stairs from the main floor living area. From the moment the family moved in, Carole Trausch was so uncomfortable in the little house that she pleaded with Jim to consider moving again. Unfortunately, he would not hear of it, so Carole set about making herself and her family as content as possible.

While Carole's feelings of unease in the house were vague and general, it wasn't long before her daughters began to voice very specific—and very odd—complaints about the place. The two older girls told their mother that someone was touching them as they lay down to sleep in their upstairs bedroom, and that sometimes their beds would shake—after which there would be a shrill beeping sound from the closet. Hoping that the sound was from an malfunctioning toy in the children's closet, Carole emptied the area completely. She did not find anything that could possibly have caused the noise.

As the days wore on, the sights and sounds of the haunting became more persistent. The presence, whatever it might be, was in the house most of the time. Carole often sat downstairs listening to heavy footsteps from the floor above when she knew her children were asleep. After a few weeks of this, the woman quite understandably began to fear that she was losing her mind. It wasn't until her sister, Kathleen, visited that Carole was able to confirm that the mysterious noises she had been hearing were, in fact, very real.

While Kathleen and Carole got caught up with one another, the two older girls were outside playing and the youngest, a baby, was having a nap in her crib upstairs. Despite these facts, the two women distinctly heard a scampering sound on the floor above. It sounded to them like the footsteps that a child's feet might make in slippers. They ran up to check on the baby, but found her peacefully asleep, just as they had left her.

By now, Carole realized that she was living in a haunted house. Worse yet, it was haunted by not one ghost, but, judging by the distinctly different sounds, at least two. It seemed the Trausch family was sharing their home with the specters of both an adult and a child.

Late in January of 1967, Carole hosted a luncheon for some neighbors. All was proceeding well until the conversation was interrupted by a piercing scream from the Trausch's youngest daughter, who had been asleep in the upstairs bedroom she shared with her older sisters. The women raced to the terrified child's side. The baby was still in her crib as she should have been, but the other bed in the room now had an imprint on it—the imprint of a small human body.

Carole picked up her daughter and started to go back downstairs with her two neighbors. Just as they began to climb down the stairs, the three women heard what they later described as "an invisible child falling down the stairs, about three steps ahead of where [they] were standing." After that incident, Carole made a conscious effort to stay on the main floor of the house as much as possible. Whatever spirits were in attendance upstairs, they never made their presence felt downstairs.

During the next few weeks, the phantom footfalls became more and more frequent. Even Jim Trausch admitted to occasionally being ill at ease in the house. Meanwhile, Carole realized that the spirits had never made any attempt to harm any of them and seemed to become more curious than concerned. Why, she wondered, had the ghost of the child never shown any interest in her daughters' toys? She didn't have any cars or trucks that might interest a boy so, instead, she put out some plastic kitchen utensils with which a child of either gender might enjoy playing. Beside those, she placed a cookie and then—as something of an experiment—covered the linoleum floor around the make-shift toys with a layer of flour.

So that she would have a witness to any developments that might unfold, Carole called in one of the same neighbors who had been over for the memorable lunch in January. The two women waited downstairs until they heard the now familiar scampering of tiny feet across the floor above them. They stayed on the lower level just long enough to be sure that the little entity had covered his usual path before running upstairs to check for physical proof of the wraith's existence.

The kitchen gadgets-cum-toys had not been touched, but the flour now had small footprints through it. Carole and her friend were both mothers of young children, so they were familiar with the pitter-patter of little feet; they judged the ones that made these marks to belong to a child about three years of age. As alarming as that final proof must have been for Carole, it was a childish drawing beside the prints that was truly spine-chilling. The little ghost had evidently stopped mid-scamper and drawn a flower in the flour in a childish hand.

Becoming bolder still, Carole brought a supply of boys' toys into the house and left them in her children's bedroom. She also spoke out loud while placing the objects in the room, assuring the spirit that no one would harm it. The toys never showed any signs of having been played with, but Diane, the oldest of the Trausch's three daughters, saw what she described as a "shadow of a little boy" not long after.

Carole had already made inquiries of the development company, asking if they were aware of any trauma ever having taken place in the area. No one seemed to know of any untoward happenings, but a family named Swanson, who lived in a unit across the lane, was also experiencing the sounds of phantom footsteps on the second floor of *their* house. These people had been so unnerved that they had, on more than one occasion, actually called the police, fearing that an intruder had somehow broken into their home.

Once, after returning from a weekend trip, the Swansons heard footsteps running across the floor above, as though running away from the people coming home. They searched the entire area, but found no one. They did, however, find lights burning despite their having been turned off before the trip—and their child's small riding toy had inexplicably been moved to the middle of the kitchen. Nothing was missing from the house and there was no sign of a break-in.

One beautiful May morning in 1967, as Carole Trausch stood at her bedroom window, she happened to look across to the Swanson's home. She knew that neither Mr. nor Mrs. Swanson was at home, yet she clearly saw an arm pulling back a window covering. As the window became fully visible, Carole Trausch was horrified to see a deathly white face peering across at her. Blinking in disbelief, Carole looked again. There was definitely a woman looking back at her—a woman with wet hair who was wearing a white nightie.

Later that day, after confirming with her neighbor that no one had been home that morning, Carole decided she would have to check back farther into the history of the land on which her house stood. First, she approached a woman who had lived on a nearby street since the mid-1930s. She was told that there had at one time been a barn on the exact spot where the Trausch unit was now located.

Still not satisfied, Carole began to probe the county records and found a puzzling report about a possibly clandestine burial that had taken place in the area in 1925. She also learned that there had been a fish hatchery business in the area at one time, and that her family's entire property had once been flooded. She connected those last two points and felt they might point to the identity of the phantom woman and help to explain her wet hair.

Feeling totally out of her depth, Carole Trausch called in two psychics. These people immediately picked up impressions of the names Fairley, Felix and Vincent. Interestingly, county records showed that families named Fairley and Felix had, in fact, lived in the area in 1925.

Even though the psychics were able to successfully convince the spirits, possibly members of one of those two families, to leave this earthly plane, the Trausch family had already made up their minds to leave as well. Living in a haunted house for more than a year had taken its toll on all of them, and they were understandably anxious to lead a calmer life somewhere else.

Unfortunately, no records exist to indicate how the Swanson family fared, nor whether the next people to live in what had once been the Trausch's haunted home ever saw or heard anything out of the ordinary. We can only hope that all those involved, both living and dead, are now leading a much more peaceful existence.

Spectral Sailors

As the following stories illustrate, not all the ghosts of old salts are able to find—or are even interested in finding—their old vessels.

In the 1960s, an old house in the San Francisco area community of Alameda was haunted by the ghost of a young Italian who'd apparently served in the U.S. Navy. The occupants reported listening to heavy footsteps echoing through empty rooms. Once, while one of the residents was falling asleep, the steps were heard walking around his bed. The man immediately turned on the light, but saw nothing. Despite this lack of a visible manifestation, the sounds continued their movement to the other side of the bed—and then stopped as mysteriously as they had started.

The concerned home owners called in psychic investigators. It was they who determined the identity of the ghost, but when their descriptions were checked against Navy records, the two accounts did not support one another. Unfortunately, that lack of substantiation did nothing to lessen the audible chaos created by the ghost of the sailor.

Six miles north of Santa Cruz on Highway 1, the ghost of a sea captain haunts a house and a nearby campground. Sightings of an old man, dressed in a raincoat and hat, are frequent enough that locals now readily recognize his description.

The phantom is usually benign, choosing to spend most of his eternity simply patrolling the grounds of the house he built in 1857. Occasionally, though, occupants of the house witness a ghostly temper tantrum as they watch ornaments flying around the room, propelled by an unseen force.

On March 25, 1930, a corpse was found floating in San Pedro Bay off Long Beach. Examination and investigation determined that the body was that of an itinerant sailor, a man named Herman Hendricksen. He had apparently died of a broken skull, most likely sustained when he fell off a pier while drunk. His remains, it was judged, had been in the water for 10 or 12 days.

Those who knew Herman were not surprised to learn that he'd gone to an early grave; he was known to be a hard-living, two-fisted drinker who frequented the waterfront brothels and bars in every city to which he sailed. Some who heard of his fate even intimated that his premature death might have been murder—murder at the hands of the cuckolded husband whose wife was having an affair with Hendricksen. If that rumor was true, then the wronged husband literally got away with murder, because no one ever pursued the matter.

It's not likely that people gave much thought to Hendricksen after his death—at least not until his spirit came back from the grave to terrorize a young woman identified only as "Ann." The exact circumstances of the ghost's initial manifestation are somewhat unclear, but we do know that the visitation occurred during November of 1988, while Ann was living in a house on 11th Street in San Pedro. The spirit explained, through a Ouija board, that his name was Herman Hendricksen and that he'd been a "transient sailor" who was murdered on March 14, 1930. He had chosen to haunt Ann's house because that is where the man who'd murdered him had lived. It soon became apparent to Ann that the spirit was both angry and aggressive. He threw things, set fires, and even wrapped the cord from an electrical appliance around a visitor's neck. Ann managed to live in the house for almost a year before moving to a trailer court in a community north of Bakersfield, far from the ocean. It wasn't long, however, before the sailor's spirit found her there and began to draw attention to himself by banging on an adjacent outbuilding. When the invisible entity hurled a visitor to Ann's home against a wall, the confused and frightened woman moved again, this time to an apartment suite on 7th Avenue in San Pedro.

That was in May of 1990, and by then the angry spirit's energy seemed to be dissipating. He was no longer destructive, but limited his ghostly activity to creating balls of ghost light—also known as ignes fatui—that would harmlessly bounce around the apartment. Because Ann has wisely retained as much anonymity as possible, we can only hope that the spirit of the murdered sailor has found some peace and, in doing so, left Ann in peace as well.

Famous Entity

One of the most famous ghost stories in the world played itself out on a quiet residential street in Culver City, Los Angeles. That is where the haunting that provided the factual basis for both the novel and movie versions of *The Entity* took place.

The terrifying events began in October of 1976, when a 35-year-old single mother of three was savagely attacked by a ghost in her own home. This woman's identity has, for the most part, been successfully protected. Over the years, in the different representations of her terrible paranormal encounters, she has been known as Doris, Carla, and Carlotta. In this retelling of the horrific events that devastated the woman's life, I have arbitrarily chosen the name Carla from the list of pseudonyms.

The phantom attacks began late one evening in Carla's bedroom when she was thrown and molested by an unseen force. Her screams of terror brought her 16-year-old son "Bill" running into the room. For a second the boy stared in disbelief as he plainly saw his mother was being assaulted. What he could not see was who or what the perpetrator might be.

Thinking that his mother had suffered a terrible nightmare, the boy tried to calm the horrified woman. Carla had her son search the house thoroughly, but Bill found no evidence of a break-in.

Sadly, these vicious attacks by a paranormal intruder continued—and Bill continued to respond to his mother's cries for help. On an evening when the entity's strength was especially powerful, its force picked the teenager up and hurled him against a far wall. He landed in a heap, his arm broken from the impact.

Until that incident, Carla had been considering the possibility that the attacks might somehow have been created by the power of her own mind—a psychic projection of some sort. Now she knew that this could not be so. Only an independent force could be responsible.

But what could that independent force be—and how could she ever get it to leave her alone?

Carla first sought help from the traditional medical community. Although a host of psychiatrists applied a variety of theories and names to what the woman was going through, none were able to bring her any relief from the manifestation. Through a chance encounter in a Los Angeles bookstore, the beleaguered woman met members of the Parapsychology Department from the University of California at Los Angeles. Under the supervision of department head Dr. Thelma Moss, a graduate student named Kerry Gaynor began an investigation.

Through all of this, the attacks continued and word of the bizarre haunting leaked to the press. The entire episode began to take on a circus-like quality. Not only were the spectral attacks continuing, but now the being was leaving scrapes and bruises all over Carla's body. The woman's pride had been totally obliterated by fear, and she invited Gaynor and his associate, Barry Taff, to bring camera equipment and spend a night in her home.

The entity was apparently not pleased by the presence of the onlookers. Cooking utensils began to be thrown about by angry, invisible hands. Cold drafts blew through the house and a nauseating odor permeated the rooms. Gaynor and Taff began taking snapshots as quickly as they could. As Carla would repeatedly scream, "It's over there," the pair would hurriedly turn in new direction and snap a photograph.

When the phantom invasion finally subsided, the trio discovered that most of the pictures taken when and where Carla had indicated the phantom was located had turned out to be totally overexposed, simply bleached out white. Other pictures featured orbs of eerie light. The photo taken as Carla yelled, "It's right in front of my face," was overexposed only in the vicinity of the woman's face; her dress was visible, as were the drapes behind her. Control photos—taken that night to establish what the house looked like under standard conditions—proved to be absolutely normal, with each one reflecting no more or less than would have been expected.

Some of those photographs were sent to the magazine *Popular Photography* for analysis by their experts. After examining the shots, the editorial board concluded that "nothing known to photography or optics ... could have explained the phenomenon."

Carla's agony went on for months and, during that time, totally ruined her life. Writers, photographers, members of the traditional and nontraditional medical communities, the curious and the concerned flocked to her home—and as they did, the entity gained strength and began to materialize with a physical form. Many witnesses confirmed the sudden appearance of a body.

The terror had reached its climax. Thankfully, the enormous strength of the terrible haunting began to wane from that point on.

Chapter 2
GHOSTS IN PUBLIC

Most lovers of ghost stories not only have their favorite stories, but also their favorite type of ghost stories. Some can be "deliciously frightened" by a tale of a poltergeist haunting an ordinary suburban bungalow. Others shiver at the mere mention of phantom lights in a graveyard. My personal favorite type of ghost story is also, by sheer coincidence, the kind I find most convincing—that of a ghost in a public place. After all, if your father always sat in a particular chair when he was alive, it shouldn't be too surprising if you or a member of your bereaved family continue to occasionally see his image there after his death.

But if two or more people who have neither an emotional connection with one another nor any particular affiliation with their surroundings report seeing the identical supernatural occurrence—in simple terms, a ghost—then this is to me convincing proof that not only does the entity exist, it exists in circumstances that are external to the observers. For these reasons, the following stories are very special to me.

Spirits of Alcatraz

The remaining buildings on Alcatraz Island are, without a doubt, the coldest places I have ever personally set foot. It's probably safe to say that anyone with even an ounce of sensitivity who has visited the site will concur.

The Miwok Indians were the first people to feel uncomfortable about the severe-looking chunk of rock jutting out of the waters of San Francisco Bay. Long before concrete fortresses were constructed to house the country's most dangerous criminals, the area natives had named the island Alcatraz, meaning the "island of pelicans"—and then studiously avoided the place, believing it to be evil. Given this history, it's ironic that people now eagerly pay for the privilege of visiting "the Rock."

The first real use of the frequently fog-shrouded island was as a strategic spot for a lighthouse designed to steer unsuspecting ships away from its rocky coastlines. Five years later, in 1859, authorities decided that the isolated location would make it a formidable venue for a prison. No one, it was reasoned, could ever escape from the remote island.

As a federal penal institution, Alcatraz was intended to house only the worst and most dangerous criminals—those judged to be beyond hope of rehabilitation. This was never a facility designed to do anything but punish the inmates and keep them from posing a threat to law-abiding citizens. As a result, many of the most infamous gangsters in American history were banished to the bleak isolation of the Rock. Al Capone, "Machine Gun" Kelly, "Creepy" Karpis, "Doc" Barker ("Ma" Baker's son) and "Butcher" Maldowitz were just a few of the best known. Robert Stroud, whose study of local birds earned him the nickname "the Birdman of Alcatraz," remains the only man ever incarcerated on the island to be remembered for anything other than villainous deeds.

Many of the guards at Alcatraz became as malevolent as the inmates, probably because they, too, were effectively isolated from civilization. The staff's often horrendous cruelty to the prisoners was brought to light during an investigation into a 1946 escape attempt. From that time until the facility was decommissioned in 1963, the population of Alcatraz steadily declined—the living population, that is. Even today, the ghosts of many prisoners continue to haunt the island.

Oddly enough, it is not just the spirits of the prisoners who died while serving sentences on Alcatraz Island whose souls remain. Some of those who died elsewhere have returned to haunt the place. Most of the hauntings take the form of inexplicable

An aerial view of "the Rock," where the malevolent phantoms of public enemies like Al Capone and Machine Gun Kelly are still incarcerated.

sounds. People frequently hear gruesome, ghostly sounds—men screaming and crying, walking or running through the corridors, whispering to the other souls who were their fellow inmates.

One cell block has been the site of so much ghostly activity that esteemed psychic Sylvia Brown was called in to investigate. An examination of her findings indicates the presence of Abie "Butcher" Maldowitz, an especially vicious man who was eventually killed by a fellow inmate. His disembodied soul, it would seem, is just as angry in death as the man was in life.

On D Block, Cell 14 continues to resonate with the sorrow and despair of a criminal who spent three solitary years in the tiny area. Today, no matter how warm the weather, that one cell remains icy cold.

The banjo-playing specter in the shower room is generally accepted as being the ghost of Al Capone. Yes, the notorious gangland boss whom the FBI nicknamed "Scarface" played the banjo during his incarceration on the Rock!

Not surprisingly, the quietest spirit in the place is the ghost of Robert Stroud—the Birdman of Alcatraz. After murdering a man in Alaska, Stroud was sentenced to serve 12 years in Leavenworth penitentiary. He spent his time behind bars studying birds and became an expert ornithologist. Shortly before his release date, he killed one of the guards and was sentenced to death. President Wilson commuted the order to life in solitary confinement, keeping Stroud alive only so that he might continue to research and write about birds—and this is exactly what the prisoner did for the next 20 years. Eventually the Birdman was released from Alcatraz, but since his death in 1963 visitors to the island have been hearing Stroud's distinctive whistle attempting to reach his beloved birds from beyond the grave.

While Alcatraz is definitely a fascinating spot for ghost enthusiasts to explore, those who choose to do so would be wise to remember that all the entities in the place were hardened criminals in life. Even Stroud, perhaps the least aggressive soul ever confined on the island, was responsible for the deaths of two people. For this reason, the "island of pelicans" is not the safest haunted place for a ghost hunt.

The Phantom Still Flees

World War I—the "war to end all wars"—had ended; the Great Depression had not yet begun. The Roaring Twenties were in full swing, and America had become the promised land where anything and everything seemed possible. Not everyone, however, was free to enjoy the prosperity. Then, as now, there were the sad few who were hostages to their pasts.

On a gray morning in 1926, the population of those unfortunate, imprisoned souls was reduced by one when the disease-ridden corpse of a 68-year-old woman was discovered in Butte, Montana. Flora Sommerton had died alone in the tiny flophouse room where she had lived for as long as anyone could remember.

That same day, more than a thousand miles away, on California Street in San Francisco's Knob Hill district, a misty presence appeared—an apparition of a beautiful young woman dressed in a flowing, beaded gown. Her demeanor suggested that she was in turmoil and fleeing from someone only she could see.

It was some time before anyone made a connection between those two seemingly disparate events, but as the frightened-looking ghost began to appear more and more frequently, details about her spread throughout the community. Older folks in the area listened especially carefully to those who'd seen the ghost. Descriptions of the formally dressed, seemingly confused entity reminded them of an incident that had occurred when they were young—the social disaster of their era.

These older people could still clearly recall the year 1876 and the formal party that Mr. and Mrs. Sommerton hosted for their 18-year-old daughter, Flora. The gathering was to be the gala event of the year. Unlike many parties of this sort, Flora's was not a debutante ball. The Sommertons were not hoping to present their daughter to eligible males—far from it. They had already chosen Flora's future husband. He was the son of an equally wealthy and established family. What they hadn't taken into account, however, was Flora's dramatic reaction to their plans. She felt no affection for the man they wanted her to marry and had become deeply depressed at the thought of spending her life with him. Despite the intensity of her feelings, the young woman said nothing to discourage her parents' actions.

Therefore, the Sommertons' plans went ahead. The party was well underway and their daughter's engagement was just about to be announced when the prospective bride panicked. Still wearing her exquisite gown, Flora bolted from the house and fled down the street. A few of the party guests tried to follow her, but the desperate young woman disappeared over the crest of a hill and into thin air.

Now it was her parents' turn to panic. Flora, whom they had always protected from the realities of outside life, was somewhere out on the streets with absolutely no resources. When their daughter had still not been found the next day, Mr. Sommerton notified the authorities. Despite widespread publicity, an intensive search, and the offer of a $250,000 reward, Flora's parents never saw her again. They died heartbroken and alone, never recovering from their terrible loss.

The Sommertons had no way of knowing that their daughter was still alive and managing to scrape together a meager existence far from the pampered world in which she'd been raised. It wasn't until her death in a Montana flophouse that anyone who knew Flora Sommerton as a young woman learned that she had lived to a ripe old age despite her apparent naiveté and lack of practical life skills.

The ghost of the young, fleeing Flora wearing a formal, beaded gown continues to appear even today. She is always seen on the same street she ran along to escape the future she could not bear to face. Sadly, no one has been able to help Flora accept her fate; as a ghost, the former Miss Sommerton seems to be in a separate dimension and therefore feels no connection to today's world. Perhaps her soul passed on to another plane the very day she died and what people are seeing is just a ghostly replay of the terrible trauma Flora experienced on the night in 1876 when she disappeared from San Francisco's high society.

If you ever have the opportunity to take the cable car up Knob Hill, be extra vigilant in watching the passers-by as you approach the Fairmont Hotel. The young woman in the long gown may not be an eccentric street person—she may be the frantic ghost of Flora Sommerton.

Records' Revenants

When I phone people who live or work in haunted buildings, I always wonder if I'll surprise them with my request for information. When Scott Armstrong—a former professional wrestler who is now an employee at Records, on K Street in Sacramento—answered the phone, it was he who surprised me. After initial introductions and pleasantries, I launched into my inquiry.

"Is the ghost male or female?" I began.

"Which one?" Armstrong asked in reply.

Among the living, the store where Scott works has long been known to be haunted, but now it almost seems as though the retail outlet's reputation as a good place for a ghost to hang out has made the rounds within the spirit community.

"It started off as one [ghost]," Scott began. "She was an elderly lady in Victorian garb. Every employee has seen her, and one of our customers was asked [by the ghost] to leave."

Scott explained that the building had originally been constructed as a hotel sometime around 1920 or earlier. "We've occupied this space for the past 12 years, but we kind of assume that this lady had something to do with the hotel."

Scott's reasoning seems sound; the store occupies what would roughly have been the lobby of the old hotel. Gertie, or Gertrude, as shop employees have come to call the ghost, keeps a particular area where Records now stores excess stock nice and cool. "When we walk in there, the temperature drops," Scott said. This, of course, is a common sign that a spectral manifestation is present.

In case anyone doubts her presence in the basement storeroom, Gertie has something of an additional trick up her ghostly sleeve. "We have a light plug-in—you know, the hanging clip light. We turned it on, walked to the end of the room, and the light was not only off but it was on the floor. It had been literally turned off and removed."

Despite the obvious inconveniences associated with working around a mischievous spirit, Scott's attitude toward Gertie seemed to be decidedly positive. "Oh, it's fun. We get a kick out of it," he affirmed.

"There's another one, a male. I'd say he's probably [in his] late 20s or early 30s. He wears jeans, suspenders and a work shirt. He was first spotted by the manager when he [the manager] was in the basement, going through some movies. No one other than employees is allowed in our basement, so when the manager saw a person walking around down there, he stood up to ask what the intruder thought he was doing. The person just walked right past him and literally disappeared."

Scott confirmed that the store manager is not the only one to have seen that apparition: "I was in the back room with a friend of mine and she saw the same ghost coming up the stairs."

Given that ghosts have been known to move things around, I asked Scott if their resident spirits have ever done any rearranging in the store.

"Sometimes," was his immediate reply. "We'll see stuff, record piles, knocked over. We've had a *Star Trek* display shoot about 10 feet across the room. I've seen videos fall off the shelf. We had a customer standing in one of the aisles who had someone grab his wrist. There was no one near him, not within 20 feet, but someone grabbed his wrist."

That same man was making use of the toilet facilities in the store's basement when, much to his shock, the door opened and closed. There was no one else in the basement at the time. Perhaps Gertrude just hadn't realized the rest room was in use.

So, in this historic Sacramento building, the living and those leading their afterlife continue to coexist.

Antique Effigy

It shouldn't be much of a surprise to learn that antique stores are frequently home to a ghost or two. Such businesses are, by definition, depositories for interesting artifacts, and the very thing that makes those pieces qualify as "interesting" often imbues them with psychic energy—or, more simply put, causes the objects to become haunted.

Such an item was housed at a store in Bodega, a coastal community north of San Francisco. The haunted artifact is a doll—or, perhaps more correctly, an effigy—of a little girl who died in the 1880s. The eerie likeness was modeled from the child's corpse and then enhanced by adding the deceased's hair and eyelashes. This mannequin was never intended to be a toy, but rather to be a comfort to the parents whose beloved child had died.

After the grieving parents had themselves passed away, their daughter's look-alike became a collector's item—a museum-piece of sorts, destined to bring a great deal of extra spirit to any venue in which it was kept. Whether the doll is possessed or haunted may be debatable, but the destruction of which it is capable is not.

The proprietor of Country Treasures, the store that came to have the doll, lived near her shop. One night, the woman's peaceful sleep was interrupted by the sound of a crash that had apparently come from the store. Half expecting to find that intruders had broken in, she ran to the door of the shop. It was locked, as were all the windows, and there was no sign of a forced entry anywhere. Clearly, something had happened to cause the noise though—and if it wasn't a burglar, then what was it?

On the first floor, the woman could not *see* anything wrong. She could, however, *hear* something. She could hear a humming vibration that shouldn't have been there. As soon as she reached the second floor—the floor where the dead child's effigy was displayed—the woman saw what it was that had made the noise and wakened her. The glass from the cabinet, where the child-like figure was stored, had cracked and broken. The proprietor's first glimpse of the effigy itself made her realize that this was an investigation that would be better carried out in daylight; with the shadows playing across the doll's usually smiling face, it looked as though the bizarre effigy was crying.

The next morning, with bright sunlight shining through the windows, the woman once again made her way up the stairs of the museum. She knew she'd have pieces of glass to sweep up, so the mess on the floor did not surprise her. What did surprise her was that the doll was now out of its case and standing alone in the middle of the room. Worse, it seemed to be staring directly at her.

After determining that her imagination was playing tricks on her, the woman began to attend to the task that had brought her to the area. Unfortunately, the activity did nothing to assure her that all was well, because wherever she went in the room, the doll's eyes seemed to follow her.

Despite considerable effort directed toward finding out where the doll is now—and whether or not it is still thought to be possessed—I have not been able to determine "the rest of the story." We can only hope that the little girl's restless spirit is finally at peace.

Office Wrecker

Much debate has surrounded the speculation of whether it's actually a person or a place that is haunted. After studying thousands of ghost stories over the years, I am convinced that both phenomena exist. Certain places are definitely haunted—the Winchester Mystery House (p. 16) or the Queen Mary (p. 148) are excellent examples that exist right here in California. There are also people who experience visits from, or sightings of, those who are deceased—no matter where those witnesses are at the time of the sighting. The cable car operator in the story "Grandmother's Ghost" (p. 114) clearly falls into that category. To add to the complexity, a further variable—an entirely different type of ghostly phenomenon—must also be acknowledged: haunting by poltergeist. This type of haunting is always associated with a person, not a place, and most often the victim is a boy or girl who is just entering puberty.

The literal translation of *poltergeist is* "noisy ghost," but those words don't begin to do justice to the power of these paranormal intruders. The entity itself may in fact be completely silent, but once it starts hurling objects around, the area a poltergeist inhabits can become very noisy indeed.

During the month of June 1964, a classic poltergeist encounter took place in downtown Oakland. An office at 1904 Franklin Street had been in turmoil for two weeks before the news of the haunting was made public. As is the case with many hauntings, the signs first showed up in devices attached to sources of electrical power. Buttons on the multi-line telephones began to light up in quick succession when there were no calls coming in. The tiny springs under the individual keys on electric typewriters became limp, twisted together and balled up.

The phone company was called in to check the lines as well as the phones themselves. Technicians could not find anything wrong anywhere in the service. A typewriter repairman, Bob Goosey, who was hired to fix the keyboards, was completely baffled. He indicated that, typically, such springs could be expected to last 10 years or more before wearing out. But for some mysterious reason, all the coils under all the keys in all the reasonably new typewriters in this one office needed to be replaced at the same time. Puzzled, Goosey took the machines to his shop in order to repair them. The man was even more puzzled, however, when he found that the machines he'd left on loan in the Franklin Street office had developed exactly the same problem. This was a completely intolerable situation because the firm in the besieged office was a court-reporting service and properly functioning typewriters were an absolute necessity.

The problems with those tiny springs were only the beginning. Soon, objects began to fly off shelves and crash into walls. It was then that the business's owners, George and Zolo Wheeler, called the police. Charles Nye, the officer who responded to their call, was completely stumped by the destruction that he found. Glass ashtrays lay in shards on the floor with their contents littered about. Moments after he entered the haunted premises, the officer watched in amazed horror as a vase, holding a bouquet of fresh cut flowers, flew off the shelf and across the room before making "a right turn" and finally smashing to the floor.

While still struggling to understand what he had just witnessed, Nye was startled by the sight and sound of eight telephones falling, one after the other, off the workers' desks and onto the floor below.

By this time, word of the bizarre occurrences had leaked to the press. Reporter Jim Hazelwood and photographer Jim Edelen of the Oakland *Tribune* arrived to cover what had become a legitimate news story. Edelen asked a transcript typist, a young man named John Onafrides, to have his picture taken while standing near some of the wreckage that the unseen force had caused. The photographer quickly set up, took the shot and then turned to leave the room. As he did, a jar of coffee creamer that had been stored on a nearby shelf moved into the center of the room and began sprinkling its contents around the office.

As owners of what had once been a successful enterprise, the Wheelers were nearing their wits' end. They had stacks of transcripts that needed to be typed, but there was no way that anyone could work in such a severely haunted office. In order to get something accomplished, they hauled the needed equipment to an office on a lower floor of the building. The next day, however, it was clear that the "office pest," as they had come to call the presence, had increased in strength and was now wreaking havoc on adjoining businesses. In both an insurance company and a denturist's office, typewriters, coffee cups and telephones were falling to the floor.

By June 16th, the situation had become completely intolerable. For an hour, reporter Hazelwood kept a log of the strange events that occurred. The longest period between notations was 15 minutes. During that hour, a part from a Dictaphone machine flew out of the cabinet in which it was stored; light bulbs exploded; a can of floor wax "fell" out of the cupboard in which it had been stored and landed eight feet away; and a metal container holding paper cups mysteriously detached itself from the water cooler, moved across the room, and began scattering cups around the floor. The room in which this happened was empty at the time, as was the room where the metal file-card box "fell" from the top of a file cabinet. A few minutes later, a two-pound coffee can did the same thing.

If people from the outside world had not previously been aware of the poltergeist in the building on Franklin Street, they certainly were after a typewriter cover flew out an open window and landed near a pedestrian on the sidewalk below. The pedestrian, a man identified as Dr. F.J. Stryble, kindly picked up the piece of equipment and returned it to the office where it belonged.

By now, it was clear that neither the police nor the press were going to be of any assistance in solving this case, so members of the California Society for Psychical Study were called in. "A classic poltergeist case" was their assessment, except that one pivotal factor was missing—the adolescent child. The psychics began to interview the firm's employees. While they did their investigation, the active spirit continued on its rampage by dumping typewriters, coffee pots, a water cooler and even two file cabinets to the floor.

Dr. Arthur Hastings, one of the psychic investigators, declared that this increase in activity was typical of "genuine poltergeist phenomenon." He added that, generally, the intensity of such a haunting would increase before subsiding altogether. His words proved to be prophetic; on June 17th, signs of the haunting in the Oakland office stopped completely.

While the atmosphere was calm, work resumed. The psychics, still surprised by the lack of adolescent in this otherwise textbook poltergeist invasion, began to center their investigations on one of the typists, John Onafrides. The 20-year-old man had recently married. Perhaps, the psychics suggested, delicately using terminology of the era, his "marital adjustments" had provided a hormone surge equivalent to that typically found in males at puberty.

Much to everyone's surprise, Onafrides immediately confessed to having perpetrated all the stunts as a hoax. Despite his confession, when questioned by a reporter a few days later, the young man acknowledged that he had not knowingly been the prankster, but had confessed only because he felt that everyone seemed to be looking for a scapegoat in order to bring some closure to the case. Onafrides felt that he was the likely suspect as the activity only seemed to occur when he was around. The man's confession, however, came nowhere near explaining why many of the strange events had occurred in empty rooms, and he retracted his confession soon after making it.

Then, on June 26th, all the ghostly activity began again. The springs under typewriter keys crumpled; glass ashtrays, cups full of coffee and even a stapler flew across the room. According to my lengthy archival search, this was apparently the poltergeist's last attempt to draw attention to itself.

This poltergeist invasion does seem to support at least a couple of theories that some students of the field have proposed. Poltergeists are not only a product of overactive hormone energy, but the person experiencing that hormonal rush often confesses to being responsible for the destruction out of a feeling of guilt for the damage he or she somehow seems to have wrought.

School Spirit

Much of the fun in visiting schools to read ghost stories to the students comes from listening to the kids—listening to learn *their* mythologies about their own worlds. Inevitably, someone suggests that the very school in which we find ourselves is haunted. Seconds later, another hand will shoot up and add, "I know that's true because I've heard that it was built over an old burial ground." While the youngsters' tales are undeniably creative and entertaining, they're simply not true—most of the time.

But when students at Gorman School, situated in the extreme northeast of Los Angeles County, start talking about ghostly occurrences in their school, it would be wise to pay attention. You see, little Gorman School *was* built over a single burial plot and it is—apparently for that very reason—haunted.

The property was farmland until 1938. Years before construction of the school began, tragedy befell the family who farmed the land. Their 12-year-old daughter, Harriet, was crushed to death by the tractor her father was operating. The grieving parents buried the child's body on the property and tried to get on with the business of living. Their attempts became more difficult and less successful over the years, so when the opportunity came to sell the land to the local school district, they seized it.

Gorman School is a compact building, housing a small student population drawn from a relatively small California community—a community where most people tend to know each other. Those people also know that the school is haunted.

The haunting centers around one classroom—the room situated directly over little Harriet's grave. Her benign presence seems to want to be acknowledged and included. One year, Joanne Yolton-

Pouder, the teacher who had been assigned to that classroom, made an eight foot tall papier-mâché tree. Her plan was to decorate it with a theme suitable to each month in the school calendar. In October, for example, the tree would reflect a Halloween theme; in November, a Thanksgiving theme, and so on. No matter what the month, there would be 19 decorations on the tree, one for each of the children in the teacher's class. It seems that the resident wraith felt left out by this tally; one morning in September, the teacher came to work to find that an additional decoration had been added by Harriet.

The ghost has also been credited with causing more than one pile of paper to mysteriously "go flying across the room." Perhaps her strangest stunt, however, took place in front of witnesses. Both student and teacher watched in shocked astonishment as Harriet's invisible hands dealt a deck of cards into four separate stacks. This was one of the times when the ghostly antics became too much to bear. Fortunately, Yolton-Pouder had already discovered that she was able to quiet the specter's activities by simply talking to her, and that was exactly what the teacher proceeded to do. Soon the phantom card game ceased.

Harriet even tried to play a kind of hide-and-go-seek with caretaker Mary Jane Fuller as the woman made her rounds through the school one day. Fuller reported that she could hear footsteps walking through the areas where she was working. They seemed to be trying to tempt her into following. Every time Fuller went to a different area of the building, she would discover that doors which should've been open were closed tight. The usually devoted employee cut her work short that night, and when she arrived for work the next day, she brought along for companionship a pet dog that she knew to be "very protective" of her. Unfortunately, demonstrating a reaction to ghosts that is common in animals, the dog uncharacteristically refused to obey its master, and no amount of coaxing would convince the terrified animal to enter the haunted school.

Students claim to be able to see Harriet—a contention that could be the product of overactive imaginations. Then again, it could just as easily be a reality owing to the tendency of children to be more receptive than adults to supernatural anomalies.

At least one adult in the Gorman community will never forget seeing the little ghost. The sighting occurred on a winter evening in the 1940s. A group of women had been meeting in the otherwise empty school. All the women except one had already made their way toward the doors to leave when the image of a little girl, about 12 years of age, appeared to the one straggler. "Don't go outside—there's danger! If you go outside, something bad will happen to you," the ghost warned. Badly upset by what she'd seen and heard, the woman rushed out of the building. In her haste, she slipped and broke her hip. Had the illusion predicted the accident or caused it? Of course, we have no way of knowing. What we *do* know is that the woman who encountered Harriet's manifestation has never been able to bring herself to set foot back in the school.

For the most part, though, the ghost of Gorman School is a popular "resident" of this California community.

Supernatural
Shopping Experience

The haunted toy store has been a staple of fictionalized ghost stories for countless years. Here in California, however, the situation is not one of fiction but of fact. The Toys R Us store in Sunnyvale, north and west of San Jose, has a long and well-deserved reputation for being haunted.

As with many ghost stories, some people are surprised to learn about this one, arguing that "the store looks too shiny and new to be haunted." But the land on which the building was constructed had its own history—and it is that history which caused the store to become haunted.

The ghost, whose activities have been well documented by staff at the store, was immediately identified by a medium visiting the site. She said that the spirit had been a ranch hand for the land's previous owner. His name was Johnny Johnson, but in life the poor soul had been known as "Crazy Johnny." He had met an accidental death on the property in 1884 and his spirit had apparently never left.

Although some workers in the toy store have been frightened by Johnny's antics, he really does seem harmless enough. Psychics who've investigated the haunting say that he is a "forlorn" soul. Despite this reassurance, employees have been understandably shocked when they unlock a store that was left neat and tidy the night before, only to find books lying on the floor and roller skates scattered about.

Occasionally, the ghost becomes a little too personal with some of the clerks—especially the young female ones. Many have complained of being tapped on the shoulder, and those with long hair have reported feeling it being stroked by an invisible hand.

Johnny is not always that quiet. He has been known to scream, "Let me out, let me out," from inside an enclosed and empty space. He has also been heard walking around in vacant sections of the store.

Unlike many ghosts, this one is a constant presence in the store and rarely lets anyone forget that he's around. He's been credited with turning on the taps in the women's rest room when no one can be seen anywhere near them. And one aisle of the store will occasionally, and quite mysteriously, smell of fresh flowers. Years ago, a staff member watched in awe as stock began flying off the shelves—not as a result of consumer sales, but as a result of a ghostly prank. (Sadly, if any of those toys were stuffed reproductions of the cartoon figure Casper the Friendly Ghost, such information was not noted.)

Despite the inherent nuisance value of having a ghost for a co-worker, employees at the Sunnyvale Toys R Us seem to enjoy the supernatural addition to their store.

Chapter 3
GHOST TOWNS

Abandoned communities are usually referred to as "ghost towns." Despite the moniker, they are certainly not always haunted; rather, they are considered to be mere "ghosts" of the lively places they once were. California's long and colorful history has left a rich heritage of ghost towns throughout the state. Happily for lovers of ghostlore, some of these are indeed haunted!

"We're Going to Bodie!"

In the late 1870s, the boomtown of Bodie—just west of the Nevada border and south-east of Bridgeport, California—was about the wildest town that the Wild West had ever seen. A late-comer to the Gold Rush, Bodie was established in 1859. Barely 20 years later, there were no fewer than 70 saloons available to serve 10,000 residents. One of those residents was a little girl who, when told about her family's upcoming move to Bodie in 1879, is reported to have prayed, "Goodbye, God—we're going to Bodie." Her statement was deemed newsworthy enough to be reprinted in the local paper, but not until the following punctuation changes had been made: "Good! By God, we're going to Bodie!"

Could this nameless little lass now be the ghost known as "the Angel of Bodie?" The spirit of a little girl is an almost constant presence at the town graveyard. When a recent visitor to the park noticed that his six-year-old daughter had wandered several feet away from him and was giggling, he became curious. Moments later, the child asked him who her new playmate was. This made the man even more curious because his daughter had never strayed from his sight and he had not seen another child anywhere in the cemetery. Judging from a description that the little visitor offered, it was quite clear that she'd spent a few minutes of her time in Bodie with the spirit of a girl who had been dead for more than 100 years.

The ghostly girl cannot be lonely in her eternity, because there is at least one other ghost in the cemetery—the ghost of a woman. Some say the lady's apparition is somewhat predictable. When she becomes visible, it is always at precisely 4:00 in the afternoon. Clad

The spirit-filled ghost town of Bodie is shown here with its tumble-down graveyard in the foreground.

in a white dress, she floats just above a particular grave—perhaps that of her husband. The most interesting feature of this sighting is that the ghost is always seen to be knitting.

The cemetery is not the only spot in Bodie where spectral presences gather; some of the 30 gold mines that once existed near the town are also haunted. In the early 1900s, an accident at the Standard Mine maimed a mule, one of the beasts of burden that labored some 500 feet underground. The miners hauled the wounded animal up to ground level, but as soon as they saw how seriously the mule was injured, they put the poor beast out of its misery with a well-placed gunshot between the eyes. After that, the phantom clanking sound of the dead animal's chains drove at least one man out of the mine forever. Six months after the mule had been put to death, miners still reported feeling—and even smelling—his presence with them at the depth where the animal had worked.

The Cain House, in the ghost town of Bodie, is still home to the phantom of the family's maid.

More recently, Walter Stone, an employee at what is now Bodie State Park, and two other men, Slim Osborne and Leslie Smith, went out to an abandoned mine shaft known as the Lent Shaft. According to Stone, "The shaft goes straight down about twelve hundred feet." The trio began to throw rocks down the opening, but stopped immediately when an annoyed-sounding voice from the shaft began chastising them with the words, "Hey, you!" All three men clearly heard the warning—and immediately took heed of its intent.

J.S. Cain was one of the original settlers in Bodie. The house he built and lived in with his family is now home to the ghost of the woman who was their maid. It is said that the woman killed herself after being fired from her position with the Cain family. Her spirit is still felt, and even occasionally seen, in the Cain House. Children who encounter her spirit feel she is a benevolent presence, but adults who've slept in the house find her to be frightening.

They say that when they feel her presence, it is accompanied by an unpleasant sensation of pressure on their chest. In addition, the distinctive sound of a music box playing has also been reported in the Cain House—when no such apparatus is functioning.

The image of a miner can sometimes be seen in the town's hotel, quaffing a beer while the sounds of a phantom pool game continue on in the background.

The Mendocini House has been reported to be haunted by the sounds of distant conversations—as though many people were talking at once—when, in reality, there was only one person in the building at the time. And even after the place has been closed down for the winter months, people have smelled wonderful, garlic-rich aromas that they swear reminds them of Italian food being prepared. People have also heard children laughing on the lawns surrounding the house.

Under a street lamp in front of the Seiler House, spirits of those who are long dead can be heard carrying on a conversation. People who've heard this phenomenon always immediately check the area, but inevitably find that no one is there.

The specter who haunts Bodie's abandoned hotel could have worked in this mill or in an area mine when he was living.

A woman has been seen at a window in the Dechambeau House, even though it was known to have been vacant every time her image was seen.

One of the strangest tales to come out of Bodie dates back to just after the Second World War. The town was all but deserted, but it seems that the few who remained were prone to over-indulging in strong drink. When a drunken man named Ed killed his drunken wife, three equally drunken townsfolk took it upon themselves to punish the murderer. After torturing Ed for a while, the inebriated vigilantes lost interest and drowned him. Weeks later, one of the three responsible for the execution was frightened half to death by the appearance of Ed's angry and menacing ghost. The manifestation, he said, glared at him and shook a ghostly fist before simply vanishing from sight. A few days later, that same man's dead body was found. No one was ever able to offer an explanation for the death except to note there was an ugly gash on the side of the man's head.

The following week, one of the two surviving murderers was found dead, sitting on a chair in his kitchen. If he had seen Ed's vengeful ghost, he never mentioned the encounter to anyone. Again, no cause of death was readily apparent. Later, a coroner examined the body and said the man had died of a cerebral hemorrhage.

Following the mysterious deaths of his two partners, the third member of the killing party was understandably frantic—even *before* he saw the murdered man's ghost. The last anyone saw of that killer, he was running through the streets of Bodie, com-pletely hysterical, shouting that he had seen the ghost. After that, the crazed man disappeared. He was never seen again, dead or alive. No one other than his killers has ever reported seeing Ed's ghost but, of course, that doesn't necessarily mean his spirit *isn't* haunting the isolated ghost town.

Bodie has been a California State Park since 1962. Astonishingly, 168 of the original buildings in Bodie are still standing. These are carefully preserved by the Government of California in what is termed "a state of arrested decay." The ghosts seem to approve. Visitors are welcome and, given the numbers of spirits remaining at the town site, anyone might be treated to a *real* look back in time, a sighting of one of Bodie's original inhabitants.

Rescue Man

The history, geography and climate of the area surrounding Lone Pine, California, have combined to create a wealth of spine-tingling ghost stories. Nestled next to the Alabama Hills, between Sequoia and Death Valley National Parks, the land is rich with natural resources. Sadly, this has meant that, over the years, the land has been both an official and unofficial battleground in one way or another. This heritage has embedded the psychic landscape with leftover energy. Such energy resonates to this day, creating a kind of temporal double exposure—today's reality laid over yesterday's. Put simply, the area is abundantly haunted.

One of the most famous ghosts from the area appears to be on an afterlife-long mission as a rescuer. Some call him the Rescue Man; others simply call him "Indian Jim." During his life, Jim was a guide and a gold prospector. As such, he knew the Alabama Hills as well as a human being could—including the rapid and drastic weather changes the area often produces. Despite this knowledge, Jim died on the hills in the 1940s, killed by a sudden winter storm.

His ghost began to appear almost immediately after his death. In those days, when Jim's image materialized it was often recognized by those who had been the man's friends. The ghost is still frequently seen but is now only recognized by descriptions handed down from those who knew him.

One of the legendary sightings of Jim dates back to the early 1950s. A tungsten prospector named George set out from Lone Pine late one afternoon to see if he could locate any pockets of the heavy metal. A few hours later, empty handed, he gave up in frustration. As George made his way back to town, the temperature began to drop and the wind picked up dramatically. Bone-weary and hoping to get out of the punishing winds, George found a secluded rock and sat down to rest behind it. Whether from hypothermia or simple exhaustion, he was soon unconscious.

Some time later, George awoke with a start. Impossibly, he heard someone calling his name. Shaking himself, George looked around. There, just a few feet from him, was his long-dead friend, Jim.

Ghost towns such as Lone Pine, California are quite often still populated by very real, very active ghosts.

"George, get up!" the phantom exclaimed to the startled man. "You must get up now and get out of here. Go *now*. Do not wait!"

Then, before the confused man's eyes, the manifestation vanished into the thin, cold air. Frightened—both by the realization that he was stranded in a dangerous situation and by the sure knowledge that he had just seen a ghost—George made his way back to Lone Pine as quickly as he possibly could. Mere minutes after his safe arrival in town, George realized why Jim's ghost had come to him. A ferocious blizzard, much like the one in which Jim himself had been tragically caught, swept through the area. For the rest of his life—with great justification—George remained convinced that a ghost had saved his life.

Since that time, Jim—or Rescue Man—has been credited with appearing to hikers who have become lost or stranded in the Alabama Hills. It is said that the ghost leads those who are in distress out of danger. Once his mission is completed and the people are safe again, he simply vanishes.

Cerro Gordo

Just east of Lone Pine lies the well-haunted ghost town of Cerro Gordo. In the 1870s and 1880s, the place was a wild west silver-mining town full of brothels and bars. Once the mines ceased being economically viable, the entire town was deserted and stood abandoned for decades, thereby creating a virtual guarantee of ghosts. Today, the remaining buildings—both with and without ghosts—are being preserved and are open for the public to explore and even to rent temporarily.

Long-dead customers continue to shop at the Cerro Gordo General Store.

The general store is believed to have a ghost, and the American Hotel is known to be extremely haunted. Here, visitors are frequently treated to the ghostly sounds of heavy phantom footsteps walking across the floor of the otherwise empty second story. Brian Richard, who was staying at the hotel while he completed a plumbing job, reported hearing "shuffling, stomping, kicking [and] heavy-booted footsteps" coming from the "creaky, rickety floor" above his head. These sounds were certainly not all in the man's imagination, because the footfalls were heavy enough to cause the window blinds to shake. Richard had brought his dog, Sandy, with him for the night and, as animals often do, the pooch reacted to the sounds by becoming agitated and growling ferociously.

Jody Stewart, who oversaw a restoration project in Cerro Gordo, took a photograph that may have captured the face of one of the ghosts in the hotel.

Ghostly guests still roam the halls of the American Hotel in the ghost town of Cerro Gordo.

Echoes of War

West of Lone Pine, ghostly battles rage. In the 1920s, passengers and crew aboard a narrow-gauge mountainside train witnessed a terrible conflict between the U.S. Cavalry and the Paiute Indians. The strangest thing about this conflict was that the fighting had actually occurred in the 1860s; the people on the train were actually seeing a spectral replay of the deadly combat.

Echoes of a similar skirmish have been heard on nearby Portal Road for more than 100 years.

Mac the Shade

Kennedy Meadows is just southwest of Lone Pine. As with so many spots in this part of the California desert, a mining community once existed there. All that's left of the makeshift town these days is a solitary ghost—and a rather unnerving one at that.

The specter's first name is no longer known because he was commonly called "Mac," short for his surname of MacSpreem. Mac was certainly not a bad man—he was merely eccentric and he liked to drink rather a lot. His death was a direct result of that habit; he was murdered in 1948 during an argument that involved the lethal combination of alcohol and guns. It's unlikely that Mac's ghost ever intentionally frightens anyone; it's just that his invisible spirit manifests itself as a rather unnerving icy coldness.

In the early 1970s, two brothers, Jake and Frank Davis, were hiking in the area with their dog. The weather was mild and they intended to camp out. When the brothers came across a depression in a sheltered area, it seemed like the perfect spot to set up camp. Although they had no way of knowing this at the time, they were not the first to choose that camp site—MacSpreem had lived there some 30 years earlier. It had also been the site of his murder and was the spot where his ghost continued to linger.

Jake was the first of the Davis brothers to encounter the phantom. He was crouched down to untie some camping equipment when a terrible chill seemed to pass right through his body. Standing up in a near panic, he looked around to see what might have caused the uncomfortable sensation. Judging by the stillness of the nearby trees, it hadn't been wind that he'd felt. Equally puzzling was the fact that Frank seemed oblivious to any unusual occurrence.

"I told myself it was only my imagination," Jake explained. So, he set about finishing the chore at hand.

The next item on the campers' agenda was to build a fire pit. Thinking he saw an ideal spot, Jake called his brother over to see if he agreed. As Jake watched, Frank started to make his way across the 10 feet that separated them. When Frank stopped and gave an enormous shudder, Jake knew that his brother had just experienced the same, strange sensation he had felt a few minutes earlier.

"What was that?" Frank blurted out. "It felt like a sheet of ice passed right through me!"

"I don't know, but I felt it myself a few minutes ago," Jake answered.

"Well, whatever it was, I'm glad it's gone. Yeah, that looks like a good location for the fire. What are you waiting for?" the older brother teased. "Get digging!"

As Jake dug, Frank collected rocks to rim the pit. The men had not been working more than five minutes when each of them felt the same icy shadow pass through their bodies.

Abandoned mines—like the one where MacSpreem worked before his murder—are common sights in the California desert.

"I've had enough of this place," Jake exclaimed. "Let's get out of here!"

"Yeah, it feels like something keeps walking right through me," Frank whispered. "I sure don't like it—and I get the impression it doesn't like us much either."

The two brothers packed up their gear in record time. Once they were safely back in Lone Pine, they began to make discreet inquiries. Before long, they were told about a little piece of local history that might have changed their camping plans if they had known about it beforehand. It seems that Frank and Jake, like many others before them, had been attracted to the spot that MacSpreem had called home. No one they spoke to had ever heard of anyone actually *seeing* Mac's ghost, but everyone was convinced that his invisible—and icy cold—soul remained at the site of his murder.

Mac seems to be merely carrying on with his life—after death—and probably has no idea that his bone-chilling presence has been spooking people for ages now. Then again, how could he know if he doesn't even realize he's dead?

Ghost Guards His Gold

The last story from this area comes from a spot about 300 yards off Portal Road—which, in turn, is just outside Lone Pine. This is where a thief buried a cache of stolen gold in 1870. For the next 25 years, the man guarded his loot, either by himself or by assigning a trusted friend to the role. Unfortunately, he was never able to enjoy his stolen wealth because authorities chose to build a fire hall directly on top of his stash! The long-suffering crook died in abject frustration and poverty. His physical body may have given up the surveillance, but his spirit evidently did not. The fire hall on Portal Road was haunted from the day it was built until the day the building was torn down in the mid-1940s.

A family named Richardson bought the parcel of land where the haunted fire hall had stood. As soon as the Richardsons' house was built, it was clear that the new building was haunted, too. Earl Richardson told a friend that he was frequently able to sense—and smell—the presence of a human being, even though he couldn't see an actual image. In a more frightening incident, the phantom leaned so heavily on Mr. Richardson's chest that the man was initially afraid that he was having a heart attack.

The Richardsons always knew when the ghost was lurking about because the air in that particular room would get very cold and the entity's footfalls could be heard shuffling across the floor. The haunting in the house was not constant, perhaps because, according to reports from Earl Richardson's neighbors the entity visited other homes in the community as well. Presumably the frustrated spirit still maintains his deathless vigil over the stash of buried gold.

The Past Meets the Present

Describing the towns of Placerville and Coloma can mean employing some strange contradictions, because these are ghost towns that are *growing*. The towns originally boomed and then emptied around the time of the Gold Rush. Today, the situation is such that ghost town photographer Dolores Steele lamented that "those little towns are growing so fast that it has become difficult to capture the traditional ghost town look on film." Ruth E. DeJauregui explains in her book, *Ghost Towns*, that such towns have "their inhabited and uninhabited 'old town' sectors." Fortunately, such activity has not noticeably diminished the numbers of ghosts in either Coloma or Placerville.

During the mid-1800s, when the search for gold was at its height, it often seemed that *everyone* was making money. Those who were not getting rich by mining the metals often became wealthy by mining the *miners*. Suppliers were particularly notorious for charging usury prices.

Phantoms from those first, wild days still frequent Bell's General Store in Coloma. When it was built in 1849, and throughout the town's boom days, the brick building was equipped with a bell above its door. As each customer went in or out of the store, the bell jingled. Today, more than 150 years later, the store still exists but the bell doesn't. It was taken down many, many years ago. Despite this irrefutable fact, people still report hearing that old bell ring as ghostly customers come and go on their own plane, suspended in both time and place.

The Wah Hop Store has also been preserved—a fact that the long-dead customers seem to appreciate. Ghostly conversations

Originally Frank Bekeart's gun shop, this structure was erected in 1852 and is the oldest building still standing in Coloma. Phantom shoppers continue to ring the bell above the door.

can still be heard, and every so often, the crack of a butcher's cleaver against a cutting board punctuates those spirited phantom chats. In real time, meat is no longer cut in the store.

The nearby Pioneer Cemetery probably deserves to be more haunted than it is. Its appearance would make a classic setting for a Hollywood-produced ghost story thriller. Sagging plots with overgrown and rotting grave markers create an inherently spooky setting. Moreover, many of the 500 souls interred therein were thieves or murderers from the town's rowdiest early days.

Given this history, it would seem reasonable to expect the area to be overrun with unsettled spirits. Not so, apparently. The sole ghost commonly acknowledged to haunt the cemetery is a calm and serene one. She is the spirit of an elderly woman. Her manifestation hovers protectively above the graves of three members of

The miner who once lived in this cabin may still haunt the ghost town of Coloma.

the Schieffer family. Markers at the site indicate that May Schieffer died in 1890 at the age of 27, Charles Schieffer was 42 when he died in 1864, and little William Schieffer only lived for two years before dying in 1861. Elsewhere in the cemetery, little Catherine Schieffer is buried. She also died at the age of two.

It's probably safe to assume that, despite the differing locations of the graves, all the Schieffers were related. It's also seems reasonable to ascertain that the ghost is somehow connected with that family. The ethereal creature, her white hair parted in the middle and tied back in a simple bun, wears a long burgundy-colored skirt that ruffles at the edges as though blown by a mysterious ghostly breeze. Seconds after she appears, witnesses report that she beckons to them, with seeming urgency, to come toward her. Those who have had the courage to follow say that, by the time they approach the Schieffer graves, the apparition has vanished.

Of course, many of the grave markers have decayed, rotted, and effectively disappeared by now. Perhaps the Lady in Burgundy's grave is one of those and her appearance in spirit form is an attempt to protest that lack of recognition.

The Haunted Vineyard House

Until recently, it would have been possible to stay a night or two at a haunted inn across the road from the haunted Pioneer Cemetery. Unfortunately, the Vineyard House is no longer in business, but has, according to the El Dorado County Historical Society, become a private residence. Perhaps now that the house is serving this more intimate purpose, the spirits in the building have been calmed.

Robert and Louise Chalmers built the rambling seven-bedroom Victorian hostelry adjacent to their vineyard in 1878. Robert, who was an accomplished man and had once held a seat in the state legislature, began to go mad not long after.

History has not been kind to Louise Chalmers, and perhaps life wasn't either. She had already been a wealthy widow when she married Chalmers. Her first husband, who had been Robert Chalmers's partner, committed suicide. Soon after her second marriage, Robert began to go insane. Eventually, his mental deterioration became so severe that he would carry on whispered conversation with himself and lie in freshly dug graves to see if they would fit his body.

It was at this point that Louise locked Robert in the cellar of their enormous home.

People passing by the Chalmers's house often reporting hearing terrible moans and screams emanating from the structure's basement. Rumors suggested that Louise completely abandoned her husband, except to deliver his meals. Others claim she treated him as humanely as she could under the circumstances. Whichever the case might have been, Robert himself decided that his wife was trying to poison him. He stopped eating the food she brought him and starved himself to death. This meant that, just as her first husband had done, Louise Chalmers's second husband took his own life.

Although there is no concrete proof to support the conjecture, the events of the next few years make a decent case for Robert's spirit having come back to haunt Louise. The vineyards stopped producing, depriving Louise of what had once been a substantial income. It soon became necessary for her to rent out some of the rooms in her palatial home. When that ploy didn't bring in sufficient funds, Louise's creditors began to assume control of her shrinking holdings. The cellar where Louise had held her suffering husband prisoner became a temporary jail for those about to be hanged. When the criminals' time was up, a gallows was constructed on Louise's front lawn.

By the time she died in the early 1900s, Louise was financially and emotionally destitute. Her once beautiful home was run down—and badly haunted. For nearly 50 years, the property fell

The Pioneer Cemetery may be haunted by the phantom of local madman Robert Chalmers.

to a succession of owners. No one stayed too long. Usually, the sounds of Robert's spirit rattling the chains in which Louise had him bound—or footfalls shuffling up and down the basement stairs—were enough to chase prospective innkeepers to another business venture. For a while, the house stood empty.

In 1956, the old place was reclaimed and converted to a restaurant and inn. The cellar that once held the tee-totaling Robert Chalmers became a bar. Revelers were often treated to the sounds of invisible taffeta skirts rustling and labored breathing emanating from invisible sources. A bartender once watched in awe as wine glasses gently—and quite impossibly—slid across the bar.

In 1975, a family named Herrera bought the Vineyard House in partnership with their friend David Van Buskirk. The new owners were confident that their experience in the hospitality industry would serve them well. The foursome put countless hours of work into the place. Gary Herrera spoke of "painstakingly choos[ing] colors and fabrics, ordering vibrant shades" only to have his shipment arrive in completely different shades than he had chosen.

Puzzled and annoyed by this turn of events, Herrera had the shock of his life while leafing through a scrapbook that he'd found in the house. It was from the Vineyard House's early days and revealed that "the colors and fabrics that had been 'mistakenly' delivered matched the original décor." The man, who had been a skeptic on the subject of the supernatural, immediately developed a new respect for forces that he could not see or fully understand.

The Chalmers's ghosts were not content to remain so subtle, however. When a young couple checked into the hotel, the man decided to turn out the lights in their room so he could play a trick on his partner. He then sat down on the bed and waited for her to come out of the bathroom. When he felt someone sit on the bed, he presumed that it was his partner and that his ruse had been effective. He turned on the bedside lamp. Unfortunately for the man's nervous system, it was not his girlfriend who had joined him but a stern-looking, bearded man! The image soon faded, but the guest recognized the face from a photograph he'd seen while checking in—Robert Chalmers's apparition had clearly not approved of the young man's attempt to tease the lady in his life.

A member of the hotel's housekeeping staff was alone in the inn when she heard the telephone ringing. She left the guest room she'd been preparing, answered the call, and, after conscientiously taking a message, returned to her regular duties. But only for a moment. There, on the bed that she'd just made, "was a definite outline of a reclining body." The woman fled from the building, returning only when she knew other staff members would also be there.

Legend has it that Louise's image has also been seen, although specifics of any of the sightings have not been recorded. Perhaps the strangest ghost sighting at the Vineyard House was made by guests who were disturbed in the middle of the night by what they thought were partiers finally arriving back to their rooms. The guests were understandably annoyed at the inconsiderate behavior and opened their bedroom door to let the noisemakers know that after-hours revelry was not appreciated. Much to the guests' surprise, three men dressed in Victorian styles stood near the top of the staircase. For a moment, the couple stared at the images in complete shock. As they did, the images stared back at the couple in equal, if not greater, astonishment before dissolving into invisibility.

Now that the house is once again a private residence, only time will tell whether the ghostly energy that permeated the building has dissipated for good.

Still Hanging Around

Just south of Coloma, the neighboring town of Placerville is also haunted. It's no wonder there are ghosts in and around the Hanging Tree Café on Placerville's Main Street; many outlaws were hanged from the nearby oak tree. Restless spirits have been known to appear throughout the town. Inside the café, spirits have actually harassed both the staff and the customers.

Like most Gold Rush boomtowns, Placerville had an official hangman. Many who have seen a manifestation in the old Chamber of Commerce Building think that the ghost resembles archival pictures of the town's executioner. The apparition is that of a bearded man with a black top hat and is usually seen looking down from the mezzanine. Because many hangings took place on that property, the hangman's association with the building is certainly reasonable.

In Greenwood, just north of Coloma, there are apparitions on the property of the old mortuary building. What was once the "hanging tree" is ghoulishly located on the front lawn of the building. Motorists have reported seeing an outline of a body hanging from the branch that would once have held the noose.

The other image that's seen there is a bit more puzzling because it isn't a swinging corpse but an apparition of a woman and a little boy. Sometimes the pair, at whose identity we can guess, walks toward the morgue before disappearing.

And so, throughout their years of abandonment and their current time of renewed growth, these California ghost towns have continued to be home to a host of historical spirits.

Chapter 4
HAUNTED BY HISTORY

California's history is an intricate and colorful tapestry—an epic tale that includes long years as a Spanish colony, the U.S. military's seizure of the territories of California and Texas during the Mexican-American War of 1846-47, and the vast influx of Yankee settlers, farmers, ranchers, and gold and silver prospectors who began to flood California around the time of its ratification and approval for U.S. statehood in 1849 and 1850. That long, rich history has endowed California with an astonishing number of ghost stories—some of the best of which are recounted here.

The Donner Party

"If I do not experience something far worse than I have yet done, I will say that the trouble is all in getting started."

When Tamsen Donner penned those words in July of 1846, the doomed woman had no way of knowing that she—and the other 86 people who made up the core of the ill-fated Donner Party— had chosen a route that would lead to unspeakable tragedy.

For several months the group made good progress on their journey from Illinois to California. In November, however, they altered their course to take advantage of a "short cut." The change turned out to be a deadly one. The group was trapped in the High Sierras by an early winter storm, and the brutal winter held them hostage in the mountains until the spring of 1847. By that time, 41 members of the group—including Tamsen—were dead of starvation or cold. Those few who survived subsisted on their few provisions, the hides of their animals, and finally on the bodies of their dead friends and relatives. There is not a more gruesome or tragic tale to be found in the annals of the American West. The traumatic suffering endured both by those who died and those who survived was so great that resonances from their experiences can still be felt in and around the area where the group wintered.

During April of 1988, a history buff named Elizabeth (her full name is on the author's files but has been withheld to protect the woman's privacy) had a memorable visit to Donner Lake and Donner Memorial State Park, both located in the extreme eastern reaches of California, not far west of Reno, Nevada. As she drove toward Donner Summit, Elizabeth felt herself becoming inexplicably excited; she later recalled that it felt "as though I were about to see beloved friends for the first time in years." Being a down-to-earth sort, Elizabeth tried to rationalize her strange

Supernatural occurrences are common at Donner Lake, near the site of the Donner Party's tragic winter in the High Sierras.

sensations by writing them off to altitude sickness—but she had been in the mountains many times and had never experienced such symptoms, so the rationalization didn't give her much solace.

As she pulled off the road at a scenic lookout, Elizabeth's strange feelings intensified. "I can smell them," she thought, immediately recognizing the lack of logic in the assertion. By that time, she realized that she had tears in her eyes and chided herself for behaving in such a melodramatic manner. She continued on her pilgrimage by visiting the on-site museum, but was puzzled to note that, although she'd very much looked forward to seeing the place, once she was actually there and looking at the exhibits, her mind seemed to be elsewhere.

Elizabeth soon left the building, giving into a strong urge to visit what is believed to be the clearing where both the George Donner family and the Jacob Donner family camped during the tragic winter of 1846-47. When Elizabeth arrived at the spot, ironically now a picnic area, she saw evidence of recent visitors—but, for the moment, the site was completely deserted. Even knowing that she was absolutely alone, the woman could not shake the uncomfortable feeling that she was being watched.

In an attempt to distract herself and to salvage something from her visit, Elizabeth decided to try to take a photograph of a tree that is thought to mark the site of George and Tamsen Donner's tent. The camera she was using had settings that adjusted automatically, as well as instantly developing film, so Elizabeth was surprised and disappointed to see that, for some unknown reason, the shot she took was badly over-exposed. To make matters worse, her unnerving sensation of knowing that she was not alone had intensified.

Now Elizabeth faced an uncomfortable dilemma. Her camera was out of film; if she wanted to get the photograph she had come for, she would have to return to her car for additional supplies. Doing so would mean having to endure the emotional and mental uneasiness even longer, and those feelings had become nearly unbearable. Fortunately, once she was off the path and back at the paved parking area, Elizabeth's mind cleared.

Before getting film from her car, the young woman stopped to use the rest room facilities near the parking lot. She could see that there were still no other visitors in the immediate area, even though she was sure she could hear someone—or something—

making noises in the men's cubicle directly beside her. When she checked, however, she found it was empty.

Determined to capture the tree on film, Elizabeth reloaded her camera and made her way back down the path. When she was once again in the clearing, her general feeling of not being alone became an acute and even more distressing sensation of being stared at and scrutinized by unseen eyes. After quickly taking the shot, the young woman paused only to honor the place and the memory of the Donner Party by tidying some litter before heading back to her car.

As Elizabeth walked back to the parking lot, her panic subsided, only to be replaced by a terrible feeling of "hollow sorrow" and utter loneliness. Fortunately for Elizabeth's peace of mind, that was her "last unsolicited emotion for the day."

Even as she penned the story of her ordeal that day, Elizabeth could not explain why she should have had such an unusual experience. She has hypothesized that it was caused by the area still being full of psychic vibrations stemming from the horrible trauma endured by the Donner Party. She also wondered if she had specifically picked up traces of Tamsen Donner's suffering. That long-deceased woman was known for her intelligence, devotion and resourcefulness. She was the last member of the Donner Party to leave the site; she sent her children ahead into the unknown while she faithfully stayed at her husband's side until he died.

Elizabeth will probably never fully understand her experience that day at Donner Memorial Park, but it certainly did make a lasting impression. "My hope is that those who suffered so much in life will not be eternally bound to the place that was their frozen hell on earth," she wrote. "Reflecting on my sojourn still fills me with wonderment—and gives me the chills."

That visitor's eerie experience at the sites where the Donner Party camped is not an isolated occurrence. James and Margaret

Reed were on the ill-fated trek with the Donners, and several stories with paranormal overtones exist about their daughter, Patty, who was a child of eight or nine. At one point during the winter they spent in the High Sierras, the little girl was dangerously weak from hunger. As Patty began to tell her father about all the angels and stars that she could see, James Reed realized that his daughter was dying and scavenged crumbs to feed her. This bit of nourishment pulled the little girl back from the brink of death and, as fate would have it, Patty Reed went on to live a long and full life. During all of her remaining years, Patty maintained that she had deeply regretted having to leave the angels behind.

Her own near-death experience gave Patty insight into her mother's deathbed vision many years later. As the older woman lay dying, she asked that the curtains in her room be closed in order to block out a bright light that was disturbing her. Those keeping a bedside vigil couldn't see any particularly strong light, but they complied with the dying woman's request out of respect. Even after the window was covered, Margaret Reed continued to see the bright light and, a little while later, she began to call out the names of the deceased loved ones whom she said were gathering around her in the light.

Patty Reed died in 1923 at the age of 85. Paranormal researcher Dr. Michael Newton believes that, in the early 1990s, he interviewed Patty's reincarnated persona. Under past-life regression hypnosis, a woman whom he refers to as "Joan Williams" identified herself as eight-year-old Patty Reed. While regressed, Joan told Dr. Newton that she was in the mountains and cold because so many of her family's belongings had to be left behind.

Joan, as Patty, further explained that Patty's father, James Reed, had gone ahead in order to get help for the stranded party. She recalled being carried out of their camp by a Frenchman and, much to Newton's surprise, when asked to name the person most responsible for their terrible circumstances, she gave him the name "Hastings." At first, this was confusing to the hypnotherapist, but further investigation indicated that the party had been advised to save time by taking "Hastings Cut-Off." This advice proved fatal to many members of the Donner Party as it left the entire group stranded in the mountains for the winter. Hastings himself had a vested interest in their route because he owned numerous trading posts along the route named for him. Since Joan knew none of these facts in her ordinary state of mind, her memories while hypnotized create a strong case for the theory of reincarnation.

Unfortunately, not all stories surrounding the spirits of the Donner Party members are terribly convincing; some even stimulate controversy. Kristin Johnson, author of *Unfortunate Emigrants*, a book about the ill-fated expedition, feels that the following anecdote has nothing to do with anyone in the Donner Party. However, writer Donald Michael Kraig, who wrote about the incident for *Fate Magazine*, is convinced it does. Whether or not the ghost story that follows is connected to the Donners in any way other than location must be left for the reader to decide.

When 40-year-old Greg Bernardo did not show up for work on Tuesday, February 23, 1993, his co-workers were surprised and more than a bit concerned. When his workmates still hadn't heard from Greg the next day, they phoned the police to report their colleague missing. An intensive search for the man began when authorities determined that his abandoned car had been towed from the parking lot of the Sugar Bowl Ski Resort the previous day. Inside the chalet, investigators found a ski locker assigned to Greg. His snow boots were in it; his skis were not. Even though Greg was acknowledged as an expert skier, all signs indicated that he was lost somewhere out on the slopes.

An experienced and skilled search party was formed immediately, but it wasn't until the morning of Thursday, February 25, that spotters in a reconnaissance helicopter caught sight of Greg Bernardo's tracks. They followed the marks in the snow until they spotted the skier about a dozen miles west of the site where the Donner Party had wintered. Greg was alive—and he had quite a story to tell.

Greg Bernardo had become lost on Monday, February 22, when a heavy fog moved in to shroud the area. Disoriented and unable to see familiar landmarks, Greg had taken a route that he hadn't intended to use. When he reached the bottom of the slope, he knew he was lost. For the rest of that day and night—and on into Tuesday—the man skied endlessly in an attempt to find help. Despite the number of miles he covered, he remained alone, lost, and in serious jeopardy.

Then, on Tuesday morning, a seeming miracle occurred. Another skier—a woman—appeared out of nowhere. For the first time since losing his way more than 24 hours earlier, Greg felt justifiably hopeful.

The woman guided the relieved skier to an encampment, where she introduced him to her friends. In return for the favor of rescuing him, the group asked Greg to spend the next day carving out a path alongside a nearby river. This he did; as soon as he was through, he called out to his rescuers to inspect the job he'd done. When no one from the small group replied to his calls, Greg made his way back up to their campsite. Nothing was there—no cabins, no people, not even any signs that people had *ever* been there. All Greg found was a deserted trail leading away from the area.

Now horribly confused and dangerously exhausted, Greg numbly followed the path before him. The shroud of fog was still far too thick for him to see where the trail might lead. He was traveling blind. Worse, the man knew enough about survival to know that his death was near. In a final attempt to avert his premature dance with the Grim Reaper, the badly weakened man struggled to use his very last energy stores to build himself a snow shelter. As he lay down against the windbreak, he wondered if he would ever get up again. Much to his surprise, he awoke and realized that he had slept fitfully for much of the day.

By Thursday morning, the snow and fog had cleared enough for Greg to head out on what he was afraid would be his last journey. He had not gone far when he first heard, and then saw, the rescue helicopter. Thankfully, it was immediately obvious to the almost fatally exhausted man that the people in the chopper had seen him just as clearly.

Days later, while being questioned about his experience, Greg Bernardo indicated that, even at the time, he wondered if the mysterious skier—and the phantom camp to which she led him— were associated in any way with the ghosts of the Donners. Whether they were or not must remain conjecture, but there are definite parallels between the events. Both parties became hopelessly stranded in the Sierras when weather obscured their path to safety. Constructing shelter from the elements allowed Greg Bernardo—as well as at least some of the Donner party members—to cheat death. Greg's description of the small settlement he happened upon matched that of one of the sites built by the ill-fated travelers nearly 150 years earlier.

Interestingly, after he had fully recovered from his ordeal, Greg Bernardo wondered if perhaps he hadn't hallucinated the woman skier and her phantom camp. Even if this were so, one must wonder if the lingering spirits of those members of the Donner Party who died during the tragic winter of 1846-47 didn't somehow influence the man's experience.

The Workers Were Dead on Their Feet

The man who experienced the following ghost sighting has no doubt been dead for many years by now. Today, we do not even know his name. What we do know, thanks to century-old newspapers that have been transferred to microfilm, and to the talents of tenacious paranormal researcher W. Ritchie Benedict, is that the anonymous man's retrocognitive experience made international headlines on January 16, 1890.

The witness to the extraordinary sighting begins his retelling by explaining that just a few years earlier, there had been a fatal explosion during construction of a "long tunnel [into] Wright's Station" (about 10 miles south of Los Gatos). Tragically, 33 laborers "were blown to the Great Somewhere Else." Although their scattered remains were initially buried near the site of the accident, some of those mutilated body parts were later disinterred and shipped back to areas the men had once called home.

With this much background, the ghost-observer-turned-reporter began his story by creating an appropriately spooky atmosphere with the old journalistic chestnut, "It was a dark and stormy night…"

During the earlier part of the evening, the gentleman in question had been visiting a neighbor's home and had stayed longer than usual. Despite the late hour and inclement weather, he began his homeward journey with determination and confidence.

"I had a good team, a comfortable buggy and an intense desire to reach home as quickly as possible," he wrote, "because I knew my family would be anxious for my appearance. The rain came down in torrents, filling the road with water and causing me to take more than usual care ... It was a few minutes after midnight when I drove near the mouth of the tunnel."

He continued, "All at once my team stood still. I plied them with the whip, but they refused to budge an inch. I held my breath and glanced around. What did I see? You may believe me or not; you may call it a fairy tale or what you will; you may term it a freak of imagination, but all the same I give it for what it is worth. I saw emerging from the tunnel 33 men attired in ghostly habiliments."

The poor traveler was badly taken aback; he had been well aware of the terrible accident that had so recently killed 33 men. He realized that what he was seeing could not logically be happening—not in his time, anyway. Those who had been killed in the blast had been so taken by surprise that they were apparently not yet aware they were dead—and their ghostly apparitions were continuing to work on the tunnel as though nothing had happened.

To justify his reaction, the man explained, "I call myself a brave man, as brave as the average male being, yet I was speechless with amazement; my feelings were indescribable. I could plainly see them slowly threading their way out of the tunnel, then, like a flash, disappear."

His justification was certainly reasonable enough, considering that he had just seen a phantom work party—a group of laborers who no longer existed. His team of horses would not budge while the ghosts were visible, but "after the disappearance of the unearthly visitors, my team started up, and unmindful of the mud, they did not stop until home was reached."

If the reader is wondering whether the anonymous man's visit to his neighbor's house on that eerie night might have included the intake of an intoxicating beverage or two—as well as the impaired perceptions that alcohol creates—the writer assured his readers that "many others who have been near the tunnel at midnight say they have seen the same ghostly march."

Spectral Silver Mine

Tales of ghosts guarding lost mines have been a staple of western story telling since the migration of Europeans into these areas. The following is a classic story of that ilk, albeit one with a more recent—and very thought-provoking—twist.

By the time the First World War ended in 1918, a small and very unusual community was developing in the gorgeous Hollywood Hills. A sometime prospector named Harvey Walton had dreams of buying a piece of that prime property and building a home there. The more Harvey daydreamed, the larger the imaginary house became—until he began thinking of the place as his "castle" and wanting it very, very badly.

Harvey was not an educated man, so his wages were unlikely to bring in the amount of money he'd need to fulfill his dream. He was also not a man inclined to criminal activities, so couldn't collect the funds by theft or fraud. No, the road to his goal, as Harvey saw it, was paved with silver—silver that the miners before him had missed.

Toward that end, Harvey Walton hired Juan Pinto, a native of the area, to guide him to the fabled Lost Mine of the Padres. The pair made the journey as far as Fort Tejon, almost due south of Bakersfield and equidistant east of Santa Barbara. There Walton obtained a pack animal, strung baskets to the beast, and began loading those containers with the provisions he reckoned would be required to complete his mission.

Thus equipped, the duo headed out again—Walton with considerably more enthusiasm than Pinto. As the men and their animal trudged along the rugged terrain, Pinto became more and more aloof. By evening, Walton realized that his companion had not uttered a word for several hours. He was concerned by this change, but dared not mention it for fear of irritating the guide he so badly needed.

Shortly after dark, the pair bedded down for the night. Harvey was in a deep sleep when something awakened him. It felt as though someone had put a hand on his shoulder—but when he looked over at Juan Pinto, the other man was happily snoring away in his bedroll, and Harvey knew that there was no other human being for miles around.

Suddenly a strange light caught Harvey's eye. The glow was about 10 feet away. As Harvey looked more carefully, he saw that it was, in fact, *two* lights—and if he wasn't mistaken, those were two fiery red eyes staring right at him! Harvey grabbed for his rifle and fired at the image. Whether he missed it or hit it can never be known. Nothing was heard to fall, and in the morning neither man could find a trace of any intruder. The noise of the blast did, however, waken Pinto, who could not even bring himself to listen to Harvey Walton's explanation.

Abandoned mines—perhaps containing undiscovered veins of precious metal—have often lured men like Harvey Walton into encounters with the paranormal.

"You'll have to go the rest of the way without me, my friend," Juan announced. "I'm not going any closer to the Lost Mine. My father used to tell me about coming to this place. He said it was guarded by a ghost. I didn't believe him then, but now I can feel the angry spirit's presence. It doesn't want us here. If you want to go on, you go alone."

Walton cajoled and pleaded, but he was unable to change the native guide's mind.

"I'll tell you what my father told me," Juan offered as compensation. "That should make you see the wisdom in my decision." Without waiting for an answer from his partner, Juan began to relate the tale that had so often been told to him. "Years ago, my father and another man were also in search of the Lost Mine. It was nightfall when they reached a spot as close to the treasure as we are now. From all the stories they'd listened to over the years, they knew they were where they should be—in a clearing beside a spring water pool surrounded by cedar trees. Like us, they couldn't go any further until the first light of dawn, so they set up camp right here."

Juan continued, "After having a light supper, my father and the other man turned in for the night. They wanted to be refreshed by early morning to complete the final stage of their adventure. They were convinced that they'd be hauling out silver ingot by the following afternoon."

"They fell into a sound sleep almost immediately and slept deeply for several hours," Juan continued. "At midnight, something woke my father. He was never sure what might have disturbed him. The woods and hills were utterly silent. He was surrounded only by complete silence and total darkness."

"His partner was still asleep," Juan said, "but father was now fully awake and alert. He strained to either hear or see a clue as to what had wakened him. At first he saw nothing. Then, in the distance, he thought he glimpsed a pair of eyes. A wild animal? No, that couldn't be the answer because these eyes were at the level where his own might be if he were standing."

The storyteller paused to catch his breath before speaking again. "My father grabbed for his rifle. Propping it against his shoulder, he took aim at a point exactly between the dreadful glowing eyes. At first he could only see that the orbs were moving toward him. Seconds later, he saw that those eerie eyes were surrounded by the shadow of a body—a body that was steadily and menacingly moving toward him!"

Nearing the conclusion of his tale, Juan continued, "The shot that should have killed his stalker appeared to have had no effect. The eyes, and now also a human-like head covered by the hood of a robe, continued toward their little camp. Then, as mysteriously as it had begun, the image stopped moving. But those eyes never did not stop glaring at my father until the moon finally disappeared behind the hills."

"Well then, he wasn't hurt was he?" Walton probed, his annoyance evident in his voice.

"No, you're right my friend," Juan replied. "My father wasn't hurt, but the beginning of a deep fear had been planted and was starting to grow. He told his companion that he'd been firing at a nearby animal, that he had missed but must have at least had scared the beast away. The next morning, the two set out on the last stage of their journey. They came to the mouth of the mine, sealed with a pile of boulders, and immediately began uncovering the entrance to the tunnel that they were sure would lead them to riches beyond their wildest dreams."

"And because they didn't succeed, it's all still there—for us to claim!" Walton interjected.

"But, wait until you hear what happened next," the other man countered. "As they rolled away the last boulder, a gust of frigid air escaped from the mouth of the long-dormant mine. The wind swept over them, chilling my father and his companion to the bone. They hesitated a moment. Both men were experienced prospectors, yet they'd never encountered a phenomenon like this before. They wondered if it was it safe to go in. After a few silent moments had passed between the two of them, they began making their way into the black hole in unison."

At this point, even a man as determined as Harvey Walton had to have been listening carefully to the message he was being given.

In a barely audible voice, Juan Pinto continued his account. "As they made their way into the bowels of the mine, the cold became more and more intense until they were suddenly forced to stop."

"Forced by the cold?" Walton questioned.

"No, my friend, not by the cold," Pinto assured him. "They were stopped by a sight that stood dead ahead of them—the sight of two glowing eyes piercing through the darkness to stare at these foolhardy men who'd dared to invade the Lost Mine."

"What happened?" Harvey demanded of the other man. "Whose eyes were they?"

Juan answered, "For a moment that seemed like forever, neither my father nor the other man was able to make out the form around the eyes. Only as the entity inched closer and closer were they able to see the rough image of a human shape. The two were frozen in their tracks, but the apparition was not. It swept toward them—and then moved *through* them as if they were not even there. The intense cold that passed through the men's bodies was something my father could never bring himself to describe. The two men knew for certain that they'd invaded what shouldn't have been disturbed. With equal certainty, they knew that the icy presence with the red eyes was probably the ghost of a miner who'd found the Lost Mine before them but had died in his attempt to extricate the valuable minerals. The soul of that long-dead miner was furious at having been cheated of his reward. His angry spirit continued to guard what he still considered to be *his* treasure."

Walton now realized that the eyes he'd seen and fired at the night before were the same ones Juan Pinto's father had encountered in the mine tunnel many years earlier.

"What did your father and the other man do?" Walton demanded.

"They fled and never went anywhere near these hills again," Pinto admitted. "Now that I'm here and I sense the atmosphere of the area, I have no reason to believe that the ghost isn't still around. I can't bring myself to go on."

"I also have every reason to believe that the same ghost *is* still around," Walton acknowledged. "Let's head home together."

The men began their homeward trek in companionable silence. Harvey Walton never did tell Juan about the vision at which he had fruitlessly fired the night before. We don't know for sure, but it's doubtful that Harvey ever realized his dream of a home in the Hollywood Hills, or that he ever again tried to locate the Lost Mine. As far as anyone knows, the mine is still rich with the silver that the wrathful wraith was protecting as his own.

Haunted Transfer Station

A dot on the map, roughly 10 miles due east of the Lost Mine of the Padres, represents a community we know today as Willow Springs. In mid-1800s, it was little more than a way station on the lengthy Butterfield stagecoach line—one of many depots where drivers could exchange their weary steeds for fresh ones before continuing on to their next stop.

But Willow Springs was somewhat different from other stopping places. For one thing, the stagecoach company had great difficulty keeping an attendant at the station after 1859. Everyone they sent adamantly maintained that the place was haunted. Considering what had occurred on the property, company officials were not inclined to argue.

A study of the informal history of the American West during that era shows that newcomers had a way of simply appearing and either establishing themselves in any given town or moving on. No matter which choice they made, most did so without sharing the details of their lives with those whom they encountered in town.

A young man named Jason Hillerson was just that sort of a stranger. In the mid-1850s, he arrived at the pretty little California town of Visalia. It didn't take long for Hillerson to establish himself. He was handsome, friendly, knowledgeable and eager to help anyone who might need assistance. In short, he was an easy person to like. Although folks enjoyed Jason's company, they also noticed that he never said anything about his past. No one knew who he had been before he arrived in Visalia—or even where he'd come from—and no one asked.

Jason Hillerman's killer would have stayed in frontier accommodations much like this ghostly hotel.

In 1859, when the position at Willow Springs livery came vacant, everyone in Visalia was surprised and sorry to learn that Jason Hillerson would be leaving their community to take the job at the isolated station. Despite his popularity, it wasn't long before most of the townsfolk had forgotten about the pleasant young man who'd been in their midst for a while. Shortly after Jason departed for his new duties, an even more charismatic stranger arrived in town. This man was very wealthy and was apparently looking for local real estate to purchase as an investment.

Meanwhile, the stagecoach stop manned by Jason Hillerson was flourishing. To a man, the teamsters looked forward to their arrival at the well-managed stopping place. Not only did the new station master always have fresh horses waiting for them, he was consistently pleasant to deal with. That's why, when a driver with a coach full of passengers and supplies made his regular stop at Willow Springs, he was quite surprised when he didn't see a team of replacement steeds tied outside the barn and ready to go.

Climbing down from the platform at the front of his stagecoach, the driver made his way into the stable and called out Jason's name. Seconds later, he looked down and saw the young man's body crumpled on the straw floor. He ran back to the stagecoach, shouting for a passenger he knew to be a physician. Sadly, it was too late for anyone to help Jason Hillerson—he was dead.

The doctor and the driver wrapped the young man's body in a blanket and carried it to the stagecoach for the journey back to Visalia. In town, the physician examined the corpse carefully but could not find any clues as to what might have killed Jason. When someone reported that the deceased had been known to go on drinking binges every few months, the doctor simply credited the death to alcohol abuse and dropped the matter.

Not knowing if Jason had any relatives, the townsfolk wondered what to do with the body. When he heard that Jason Hillerson's remains might be unceremoniously dumped in a pauper's grave, the wealthy real estate speculator offered to pay for a proper service. A few days later, with most of the town's citizens present, Jason Hillerson's body was formally laid to rest. By the end of the week, the generous benefactor had quietly left town, but few, if any, of the people of Visalia connected the two events.

Jason Hillerson's death left the station at Willow Springs in need of an attendant. As that situation could not be tolerated, the stagecoach line quickly hired as a replacement a man who had known the deceased employee—a man we'll call Frank.

Frank was settling in nicely to his secluded posting when, on the second evening of his assignment, he was relaxing in the kitchen of the small company-supplied house. As he idly gazed out a window, Frank thought he saw a pair of eyes staring in at him. Knowing that there was no one for miles around, the man rubbed his eyes and gave his head a shake, thinking that he was perhaps a bit lonelier than he wanted to admit. Seconds later, the eyes vanished, leaving Frank with the distinct feeling that his imagination had been playing tricks on him.

Even so, Frank thought he should check the stables for possible intruders. After all, he was new to these responsibilities and wanted to do a good job and make a favorable impression on his employer.

The moment he walked into the rough out-building where the horses were kept, Frank was glad he had come. The poor animals were extremely agitated. As there was no readily apparent cause for the horses' distress, he presumed that they were ill and began rubbing them down. Just then, a movement in the corner of the stable caught his eye. Turning his head to get a better view, Frank clearly saw Jason Hillerson—the man whose funeral he'd attended only the week before! Worse, this sighting was not a fleeting thing. Frank watched in paralyzing horror as a man he knew for certain to be dead tended to one of the other horses in the stable. Seconds later, Frank fled from the barn to the safety of the nearby house.

Once he'd calmed down enough to catch his breath, Frank knew that he had seen a ghost. He realized that, even though Jason's image had been quite clearly defined, it had also been transparent—Frank had been able to see the rough hewn timber walls *through* the man in the stables.

Poor Frank was badly conflicted about to what to do. The horses had also been spooked by the ghost. He did have a responsibility to look after the animals, but he was too frightened to venture near the out-building again. After trying to talk himself into going to the horses—and not succeeding—Frank packed his bags, rode directly to his employer's house, and quit his job. As he left the surprised man's house, Frank made a statement that would have far-reaching implications. "I think Jason Hillerson was murdered," he declared. "His spirit's not at rest because his killer has succeeded in getting away with murder."

However, the owner of the coach lines had more immediate concerns. He had to get the Willow Springs station manned before another stage came through in a few days. But by the time he started looking for recruits, word of Frank's terrifying experience had spread like wildfire and no one wanted to work in a station that was said to be haunted. The eventual solution was not only expensive but, as it turned out, far from permanent. Two men offered to accept the assignment—as long as they could go to the outpost together. Not seeing that he had any alternative, the company owner agreed.

Unfortunately, even the extra expense of hiring two men didn't solve the problem. Despite their initial bravado, Jason's ghost chased the new employees away almost immediately. People began to refer to the area as "Haunted Springs" and started discussing what could be done to exorcise the restless spirit. More and more people wondered if Frank's assessment hadn't been the correct one. Maybe Jason Hillerson *had* been murdered—and perhaps his spirit would not leave the station until the killer had been found and punished. Others asked how that could possibly be the case when the doctor who had examined the corpse had not found even minor injuries.

The mystery was not solved until the autumn of 1872, when it came to light that the wealthy stranger who'd paid for Jason Hillerson's burial was, in fact, Robert Hillerson—Jason's younger brother. Their father, an extremely wealthy Scotsman, had willed his entire estate to Jason. Robert received nothing unless Jason died first; Robert would then be the next-of-kin and therefore the benefactor. In order to make sure that this was how the events played out, Robert had borrowed money and searched tirelessly until he found people who knew his brother's whereabouts.

Once Robert determined that Jason was alone at the transfer station, the scheming man knew what to do. He rode out to Willow Springs, gave his brother a warm greeting, and offered him a drink to celebrate their reunion. Because Jason was known to be fond of whiskey, Robert was sure he would drink it quickly. He was right. While Robert pretended to sip on his drink, Jason quickly emptied a full glass of poisoned liquor. Seconds later, the older brother collapsed. Before the hour was out, he was dead.

Robert carried Jason's body out to the stable, laid it down on the dirt floor, and rode back to Visalia. Once there, he only had a day or two to wait. Shortly after paying for and attending Jason Hillerson's funeral, Robert left town on a train bound for New York City. From there, he took a ship back to Scotland, hired a lawyer to request a copy of Jason's death certificate from the State of California, and sat back to collect his riches.

Robert Hillerson just might have gotten away with murder if it hadn't been for his brother's determination even in death to see that justice was done. Jason's ghost appeared so frequently and frightened so many people that it became a story worthy of newspaper coverage. People began to speculate about why the man's soul had not gone on to its final reward. Perhaps Jason didn't die of natural causes, they speculated; perhaps he was murdered. The idea took hold and inquiries were made. Soon everyone knew that the affable stranger who'd been so loose with his money, even paying for the funeral of a man he supposedly had never met, had, in fact been Jason Hillerson's brother—and his murderer.

As soon as charges were laid against the younger man, the ghost of Willow Springs vanished for good.

The Walnut Girl

West of Jason Hillerson's grave in Visalia lies the tiny town of Armona. It was here that, for many years, a train station stood abandoned and haunted by a pitiful and poignant little ghost. The ghost was that of a girl who had needlessly died at the age of nine almost a century earlier.

It seems that the little girl and a few of her friends had dared one another to bathe naked at a swimming hole just outside town. As they giggled noisily, enjoying their "skinny dip," the girls attracted the attention of a group of boys who had been playing nearby. In what turned into a deadly game, the boys threatened to come into the water after the girls. Most of the bathers fled to a nearby walnut orchard, but one little girl was too frightened to move. Instead, she ducked her head under the water in a desperate attempt to make the boys believe that she too had vanished into the forest. Sadly, the terrified girl drowned.

The pitiful little spirit roamed the area for years. She came to be known as the Walnut Girl because she was always seen where walnuts were grown, stored or sold. No male ever saw the ghostly manifestation, but girls around the age of nine frequently caught a glimpse of the naked apparition.

Orbs of eerie ghost light—such as those frequently reported at the abandoned Visalia train station—are easily photographed by today's high-tech digital cameras.

The ghost was also seen near the train station where, at the height of the Great Depression in the 1930s, hoboes would frequently report seeing lights shining through the broken windows. Of course, anyone familiar with the area knew that the station had not been used for years and figured that those who saw the lights were suffering from overactive imaginations.

Responding to reports of mysterious lights, authorities would frequently drive out to check on the old station. They inevitably found it deserted, just as they had expected it to be. In order to prove the point that the wild tales of transients were not to be believed, the police even took photographs of the severely dilapidated building. To further document that the pictures were, in fact, taken at the old train station, the men decided to note compass readings in the exact location.

Unfortunately, they were unable to do that because the needle of their compass was malfunctioning. No matter how many angles the men tried, the compass would simply not point north. Disappointed and puzzled, the officials resigned themselves to the limits of their investigation—and to the photographs being proof enough that there could be no light shining from the building.

When the photos of the train station were developed, everyone noted that they were of poor quality. There were random spots of light sprinkled throughout every frame. Only from the privileged perspective of today, some 70 years later, are we able to tie all the events together. The little girl's ghost was likely the energy that caused the men's compass to fail and created the mysterious spots of light on the photographs.

With today's highly accurate digital cameras, these sorts of luminous anomalies show up in more and more photographs. These orbs, as they are commonly called, are becoming recognized as signs of supernatural entities being present. The strange photos at the train station were taken in the 1930s using the rudimentary technology of that day. The limitations of early photography makes the presence of spots of light on the film quite astounding and unusual. Today, many students of the paranormal would accept the old pictures that were once thought to be of poor quality as photographic proof of a ghostly presence.

Grandmother's Ghost

Imagine how dangerous it would be if the grip man on one of San Francisco's Powell Street cable cars suddenly saw a ghost. A newspaper report that made headlines as far away as Kingston, Ontario declared that this is exactly what happened on August 18, 1888. John Edward Hills, described as being "an intelligent Englishman, 26 years old" had quite a tale to tell—a tale that is best told in his own words.

"For two months," Hills began, "I've been a grip man on the Powell Street road [sic]. Last Sunday, while handling the lever I was startled on seeing the apparition of my grandmother, dressed in fantastic garb, dancing along about four rods ahead ... I rubbed my eyes and looked a second time, for the old lady has been dead for four years and was buried near London. There she was, though, and I saw her as plain as I see you now. As I kept on looking at her my head began to whirl and I was seized with a strange desire to run over her. But she kept out of danger and in the chase several persons on the street narrowly escaped being knocked down by the car. Finally the apparition disappeared."

But the ghost of the old woman was not ready to leave her grandson alone just yet. According to Hills, she appeared in his room and "talked to me in the voice that I remembered well." In response to the specter's words, the distraught man tried to flee, but "at the bottom of the stairs [I] met my ethereal visitor. She beckoned me. I followed her down Broadway, and continuing on that street we came to the wharf. She sailed out on the water and I jumped in. She grinned and kept on beckoning me. Being a good swimmer, I kept on until the phantom disappeared."

The man was a good way from shore and exhausted. "I was picked up by the tug Monarch, put to bed and given a good dinner. No sooner had I landed on shore than the old lady again paid me a visit."

By this time, the press had heard of the strange sighting. A reporter interviewed Hills and learned that he had been his grandmother's favorite and a likely person for her spirit to visit. What confused and upset Hills was her after-death demeanor. "She was a dignified old woman ... why should she appear so horribly dressed and make such grimaces I am unable to tell."

From here we must each write our own ending to this internationally reported ghost story, because there were no further reports about either grip man John Edward Hills or his grandmother's grimacing ghost.

Chapter 5

THE SPIRIT'S INN

Hotels, motels and inns serve the traveler as a temporary home away from home. Therefore, it shouldn't be too surprising to learn that just as houses are frequently haunted, many of these temporary lodgings also have resident ghosts.

As the next few stories demonstrate, these hostelry-based spirits—like ghosts anywhere— range from those that are barely noticeable to those that are a terrible nuisance. The ghosts, like the hotels they haunt, can also range from the very famous to the considerably more obscure. Furthermore, there is a tremendous range in the attitudes hotels have about their ghosts; some hotels are very accepting and even protective of their spirit residents, while others discreetly designate any haunted rooms "DNR"—which stands for "Do Not Rent." Still other places are completely closed-minded about the matter and deny outright that they are haunted—whether they have ghosts or not. Fortunately, for lovers of ghostly tales, occupants of that category are few.

Kate's at the "del"

The Hotel del Coronado, located on the western boundary of California's San Diego Bay, is one of the world's most spectacular and luxurious hotels. Its classic Victorian architecture and unparalleled ocean vistas are so incredibly photogenic that the hotel was the site of extensive location shooting for director Billy Wilder's classic 1959 comedy *Some Like It Hot*, starring Marilyn Monroe, Jack Lemmon and Tony Curtis. By happiest coincidence, the "del"

Marilyn Monroe greets her fans during the 1958 filming of Some Like It Hot *at the Hotel del Coronado. Interestingly, Marilyn is thought to haunt a different California hotel—the Hollywood Roosevelt (see next story).*

Guests at the Hotel del Coronado relax and enjoy the ocean view, circa 1892, the year of Kate Morgan's death.

is also home to one of the world's most intriguing and mysterious ghost stories.

On Thursday, November 24, 1892, Kate Morgan checked in to the del under the pseudonym Lottie Anderson Bernard. The following Tuesday, the once-beautiful young woman was found dead on a staircase outside the hotel. A single bullet lay buried deep in her head. Kate Morgan's spirit has remained in residence at the Hotel del Coronado ever since.

Immediately following Kate's death, mystery, scandal and rumor swirled around the tragedy. Within a week, facts began to unravel parts of the puzzle—but it took a painstaking investigation by an experienced and determined researcher, nearly a century later, to finally determine that the death had been a murder rather than a suicide as was initially thought. Despite that tenacious examination by lawyer Alan May and the additional facts it revealed, there is much about this ghost story, and even the ghost herself, that will always remain a mystery.

The woman who was to become Kate Morgan was born on September 23, 1865; she was George and Elizabeth Farmer's second daughter. The delivery was a difficult one and Elizabeth lived less than an hour after her daughter's birth. That death was the first in a series of tragedies that would follow the girl throughout her life—and even after her death.

George Farmer was unable to cope with the loss of his wife and the sole responsibility of raising his daughters. He began to drink heavily. Fortunately, the children's maternal grandmother stepped in and took over most of the child-rearing duties. From that point on, George's most significant contribution to Kate's development was to teach her how to play poker.

On December 30, 1885—a week after meeting him at a poker game in her father's house—Kate married a handsome young medical student named Tom Morgan. The newlyweds settled in with Tom's family, and Kate was as happy as she'd ever been. The following November, their son was born. But for Kate, tragedy lurked even behind that joyful event; the infant died shortly after birth. Devastated by the loss of the baby, the young couple resolved to reinvent themselves and their lives.

The end had begun.

Combining Kate's alluring beauty and Tom's ability as a card shark, the pair began to travel across the country. They rode one train after another, either initiating or joining high stakes poker games. Kate, posing as Tom's sister, would flirt with the other players to distract them from the card game, thereby ensuring that Tom would come away the winner.

The pair worked this ruse, with varying degrees of success, for the next three years. By that time, Kate was pregnant again and wanted desperately to settle down. Unfortunately, Tom had no such desire. The couple had a heated argument, and Kate Morgan fled from her husband when the train they were riding stopped in San Francisco.

Pregnant and alone in a strange city, Kate gratefully accepted when a minister and his family took pity on her and welcomed her into their home. When the baby boy was born on Christmas Day in 1889, the minister and his wife gave the child their last name and began to raise him as their own. If anyone asked, the kind couple would explain that Kate, whom they called "Audrey," was the baby's cousin. It's not likely that anyone did ask, though, because less than a week after her son's birth, Kate was back riding the rails with Tom.

When Kate became pregnant for a third time, she finally told Tom that they *must* settle down. After another argument, he apparently agreed and sent her ahead to Southern California. So it was that, on November 24, 1892, Kate Morgan—pregnant, distraught and alone—checked into the Hotel del Coronado as Lottie A. Bernard.

The luxurious hotel had only been open for four years but had already established a sterling reputation; then as now, their guests' comfort was of paramount importance. Many people on staff remembered noting how unwell "Lottie" seemed, and several offered to arrange for whatever medical help she might need. Kate rebuffed all offers of assistance. The last time she was seen alive, Kate was wearing a shawl over a black lace dress and dabbing at her eyes with a hanky. At 8:30 the next morning, Kate Farmer Morgan's lifeless body was found on an outer staircase leading to the beach.

As soon as the authorities tried to notify her next of kin, they realized that Kate had used a false name. Rumor, innuendo and gossip spread faster than a storm moving across the bay. A coroner's inquest determined that the woman's death had been the result of a "pistol shot inflicted by her own hand with suicidal intent."

Local reporters, however, suspected that there was considerably more to this case than had been discovered up to that point. In the December 8, 1892 issue of the *Los Angeles Daily Times*, a scribe

375

CERTIFICATE OF DEATH. ✓ 188

CORONER'S OFFICE,
CITY AND COUNTY OF SAN DIEGO.

San Diego, Cal. *Dec 12* 1892.

Name *Mrs Kate Morgan*

Aged *24* years, ~~Male.~~ Female.

Occupation ———— Married. ~~Single.~~ Widow. ~~Widower.~~

Place of Birth State or Country *Iowa* Nationality *American*

How long resident of this City or County, *4 days* years.

Previous Residence, *Los Angeles* Race *White*

Place of Death, *Coronado Beach*

Date of Death, *November 29/1892*

Date of Burial, *December 13th 1892*

Place of Interment, *Mt Hope* Cemetery.

Johnson's Undertaker.

CORONER'S CERTIFICATE.

I. *M. B. Killar* Coroner, do hereby

Certify, that having made all needed examination and inquiries on the body of above described decedent, I do hereby certify, that *Mrs Kate* came to *her* death in this *County* by *a pistol shot inflicted by her own hand with suicidal intent*

M. B. Killar.
Coroner, City and County San Diego.
By *H J Stilson* Deputy Coroner

The death certificate of Kate Morgan, who died under mysterious circumstances at the "del" and still haunts the elegant hotel.

penned the following provocative phrase: "Dark mystery surround[s] the suicide of unknown girl at the Coronado Hotel." Meanwhile, because no one came forward to claim it, Kate Morgan's body was hastily buried in a poorly marked grave on December 13, 1892.

Evidence that Kate's restless spirit was haunting the hotel began almost immediately and continues even today. Some witnesses and paranormal investigators are also convinced that a second ghost, that of a hotel maid who disappeared immediately after Kate's funeral, is also in residence. There is no hard evidence that the maid's disappearance was connected with Kate's death; there isn't even any proof to indicate that the maid died. She may well have merely left her job, and the area, without advising anyone. Despite these intangibles, those who hold to the theory of the second ghost speculate that, in the last few hours before their deaths, Kate's and the maid's lives were intertwined.

Supporters of this premise point out that many people have reported feeling inexplicable cold spots and hearing strange gurgling sounds in a small, oddly-shaped room that is thought to have served as a maid's quarters during the early days of the hotel.

Because Kate's image has actually been seen, she is easy to identify. Most often her ghost either floats through the hotel's hallways or stands at a window, looking out as though watching for someone. Her presence is also credited with causing both telephones and televisions to malfunction. While those tricks are accepted as routine ghostly activities, Kate's ghost has also been credited with one rather amazing accomplishment—that of directing an investigation into her own death, nearly 100 years after she was buried.

In the summer of 1989, Alan May, a San Francisco lawyer, surprised himself by becoming thoroughly obsessed with both Kate Morgan's life and death. He embarked on a year-long study of the case. At the end of his investigation, May had not only found

The specter of Kate Morgan is frequently spotted in the "del's" hallways or standing at a window.

convincing evidence that the young woman's death had been murder rather than suicide, he had also turned up proof that he himself was Kate Morgan's great-grandson! The chain of events which led May to that conclusion began with a casual remark from a colleague to the effect that there was a ghost at the Hotel del Coronado. That comment, intended only as a bit of light-hearted conversation, was enough to send Alan May on an amazing genealogical odyssey.

In *The Legend of Kate Morgan*, the book May wrote about his experiences and findings, he describes his stays at the Hotel del Coronado in detail. He explains how the ghost of the long-deceased young woman came to him and directed his investigation. Determining that Kate's death was not a suicide was a relatively simple matter for someone trained to follow clues relating to legal and criminal matters. The bullet that killed her didn't match the gun she was found holding; the angle at which the bullet entered her head would not have been possible from a self-inflicted gunshot; and a suicide would have made it virtually impossible for her body to have fallen into the position in which it was found. With very little effort, Alan May came to the undoubtedly correct conclusion that Kate Morgan's death was an unavenged murder.

The Hotel del Coronado, with its classic Victorian architecture and magnificent ocean vistas, is home to two ghostly women.

Puzzled by his fixation with a very old murder, Alan May began to pay even more attention to the hints and suggestions that his ghostly visitor was leaving for him. After checking with his family's unofficial historian, May was shocked to discover that his grandfather, Alan Mayer May—the man whose name he himself bore—was the baby boy whom Kate Morgan had left with the minister's family before she rejoined her husband in his traveling poker scam. Kate Morgan was, therefore, Alan May's great-grandmother. No wonder her restless spirit had chosen him to solve the mystery!

In the late summer of 1990, when Bev and Gerry Rush decided to spend a very special weekend together, they chose the Hotel del Coronado. Shortly after they had settled into their room, a bellman came to tell them that an error had been made and they'd been assigned the wrong room. In order to make up for the inconvenience of having to move, the Hotel offered the Rushes a complimentary bottle of champagne.

What happened later that night and the following day seemed to indicate that the ghosts at the del were not quite finished directing examinations about themselves and the circumstances of their deaths.

During their first night in the hotel—at a time which Gerry Rush later estimated to be between 2:00 and 3:00 AM—a sound from the hallway just outside their room jolted him awake. He was sure that he'd heard a woman crying—so sure, in fact, that he hastily pulled on a pair of shorts before opening the door and peering out into the hall. There, crouched on the floor and weeping, was a woman dressed in a maid's uniform.

When Gerry Rush asked the distraught woman why she was crying, she told him that she'd been murdered. The exchange left Rush badly confused. He closed the door and went back to bed. The next morning, he thought that he'd merely had a strange dream—perhaps as a result of imbibing too much champagne just before bedtime—until he found that the shorts he remembered donning before opening the door were lying in a heap just inside the doorway.

As the Rushes got ready to begin their day, Gerry was still disturbed by what had happened in the night. Even if the encounter had only been a dream, he couldn't shake the slightly discombobulated feeling he was experiencing. For that reason, Gerry mentioned the episode to the hotel employee who had helped them change rooms. The bellman suggested that Rush look for a copy of the book about Kate Morgan, the hotel's resident ghost.

At this point, even more "coincidences" fell into place. As soon as he saw the book, Gerry was astonished to realize that not only had he and the book's author served in the Army together, but Alan May had actually saved Gerry Rush's life in Vietnam. Rush's search for the sobbing woman's identity was then immediately replaced by his search for his old Army buddy.

That search was a simple one, and after becoming reacquainted with Alan May, Rush and his wife finally read the book that May had written about Kate Morgan. By the time he turned the last page, Gerry Rush was convinced that the specter he had heard and seen outside his door that night at the del was the ghost of the maid who had disappeared at the time of Kate Morgan's death. Knowing that the Rushes would reach Alan May with this additional evidence about her own long-ago murder, the spirit of the maid made certain that the couple would spend the night in a room where her spirit would be strong enough to manifest itself to them. That was apparently the murdered maid's way of ensuring that her story would also be told.

Alan May died in 1992, 100 years after the death of the woman who was his great-grandmother. By the time he passed away, May had not only made certain that Kate Morgan's story was told publicly but had also seen to it that her grave was properly marked.

After his death, the Rushes released a revised and expanded edition of May's book, now titled *The Legend of Kate Morgan: The Search for the Ghost of the Hotel del Coronado*, in which they append the sad tale of the maid's demise to Kate's already poignant story.

Despite the fact that their stories have now been told, there is no indication that either the ghost of Kate Morgan or that of the missing maid have left the Hotel del Coronado. But then, who could blame these spirits for lingering? Why would anyone leave such a wonderful place if they could stay forever?

Home of the Stars— Dead or Alive

The Hollywood Roosevelt Hotel has a refreshingly open attitude about their ghosts. Some years ago, administration at the hotel drew up an eight-page collection of ghost stories. The information was "originally compiled for the entertainment of the staff"; even so, the booklet advises all employees, "If anyone asks you whether the Hollywood Roosevelt is haunted, the answer is YES!" More recently, those spooky tales have been made available to the general public on the hotel's Website (www.hollywoodroosevelt.com), which contains brief descriptions of the hauntings at the hotel under the tactful heading of "Tall Tales."

The Roosevelt played in important role in the lives of many legendary movie stars. To a large degree, Hollywood's hotel and film industries grew up together. The hotel had only been open for two years when it hosted the very first Academy Awards ceremony in

The historic Hollywood Roosevelt Hotel was the site of the very first Academy Awards ceremony. Today it is the site of an uncommonly large number of active hauntings.

1929. Since then, the palatial inn has hosted many glittering, star-studded parties and has long been regarded as *the* place to see and be seen. As often happens, the intensity of emotion experienced over the years by those anxious to be recognized at the hotel has left the grand old hostelry uniquely stocked with echoes from the past.

The only slightly surprising element to this haunted "house" story is that the ghosts were apparently not officially acknowledged until 1985, just prior to the hotel's grand reopening after a mammoth two-year, $40-million renovation. During mid-December in 1985, everyone at the Roosevelt was busy preparing for the upcoming day when the hotel would once again receive guests. No matter what their usual duties or job titles, all employees were directly involved with the last-minute details—secretaries were sweeping, bellmen were dusting, waitresses were helping make up guest rooms. The place was a veritable model of industry.

Alan Russell, personal assistant to the general manager, was painstakingly sweeping the floor of the Blossom Ballroom in anticipation of the new carpet being installed. Like many of those on staff, Russell was a part-time actor; given the star-studded history of the hotel, the "day job" was very much a labor of love. Being able to devote some of himself to this gorgeous room that had been so important to the history of movie-making felt more like a privilege than a chore. It was also a perfect time, he thought, "to commune with the spirits of those who received Academy Awards here."

As Alan's experience unfolded, it became a far closer encounter than he had anticipated. The room is large and the job had to be done thoroughly, so Alan was taking his time and making sure he didn't miss any part of the floor. After repeatedly going back over to a certain area in the ballroom, he realized that while the rest of the room was kept at a very comfortable temperature, the air in that particular spot was incredibly chilly.

More puzzled than concerned, Alan called in a fellow employee, Kelly Greene. He hoped that together they could determine what was causing the anomaly. They didn't succeed in finding an explanation, but they did document the strange physical properties of the area. The cool spot is a circle about 30 inches in diameter, in which the temperature is inexplicably 10 degrees cooler than any-where else in the room. Every logical cause for this oddity was checked, but to no avail. Since then, visiting psychics have explained that the cold spot is caused by the ghost of "a man wear-ing black." The psychics added that they detected "a lot of anxiety" in that one small area.

While Alan Russell was puzzling over the strange situation in the ballroom, another employee, Suzanne Leonard, was dusting in the general manager's office. One of the pieces of furniture in the office was a tall, dark-framed mirror. As Suzanne wiped her cloth over the reflective glass, she was shocked to see the face of a young blond woman staring back at her. Suzanne had assumed that she was alone in the room, so she swung around to see who had joined her. There was no one else in the office, and therefore no way that anyone's face could've been reflected in the mirror. She turned back to the mirror. The image was still there.

That was enough for Suzanne! She left her chore and went in search of the man whose office she'd been cleaning. According to information released by the hotel, the general manager "told her that the mirror had belonged to Marilyn Monroe and had been removed from the suite out by the pool that Marilyn had often occupied." While those in authority at the hotel are understand-ably hesitant to state that the long-dead movie legend haunts the mirror, they do report that "two psychics have 'read' the mirror and told of seeing great sadness [in it]." Management has since moved the mirror to a spot where it is more accessible to visitors. They invite those passing to "take a look—you may see a blond reflection." (When psychic Peter James investigated that same mir-ror, it revealed a "pretty, dark-haired woman" who gave her name as Dee Rio, but the image vanished before he could learn anything about her.) Marilyn Monroe's presence in the hotel is not restricted to sightings in the mirror. The sex symbol's image has also been detected by the pool that is located near the Tropicana Bar. It is also said that Betty Grable, Gypsy Rose Lee and Ethel Merman have left their psychic imprints in that part of the hotel.

Before the Roosevelt's reopening, more than just the Grand Ballroom and the manager's offices had to be cleaned. Guest rooms also had to be readied for occupancy, and that is what a team of workers was busy doing on the ninth floor when a woman who usually worked as a waitress in the hotel's dining room had a paranormal encounter. At first, she didn't recognize it as such—she thought that the rather sudden cool breeze she felt in Room 928 was only a draft. After all, there were others working up on that floor, and it was perfectly reasonable to think that one of them might have left a door or a window open near that room.

The woman put the incident out of her mind until she walked back into the room to stock it with towels. As soon as she stepped inside the room, the door forcefully slammed shut behind her. Not only was this startling, but the implications were also extremely unnerving to the woman—she knew for a fact that the doors to *all* guest rooms in the hotel operated on compression hinges, making it physically impossible for any of them to slam. Even so, she knew what she'd heard.

Understandably anxious to have other people near her, the woman rushed out into the hallway. As she did, she felt the cool draft again; then, while making her way down the hall, she felt something ice cold brush past her. This woman was no doubt thankful that her usual waitressing job with the hotel would rarely, if ever, require her to be in Room 928 again!

Two other female employees didn't have that luxury. After explaining to their supervisor that they felt "something strange" in Room 928, the pair absolutely refused to enter the room ever again.

Hotel records show that Montgomery Clift rented Room 928 while he was filming the classic movie *From Here to Eternity*.

During those months, he apparently had a habit of pacing up and down the corridor while memorizing his lines. What a shame that the hotel workers who were so startled couldn't have known they were possibly in the presence of one of the most handsome movie stars the world has ever known—they might have felt honored rather than frightened!

Despite these bits of interference from beyond, the Roosevelt Hotel reopened for business in a limited capacity just before New Years Eve in 1985—only rooms on the third, fourth and fifth floors were ready for occupancy. For this reason, the hotel's switchboard operator was surprised to receive a phone call, at exactly midnight, from a room on the tenth floor. The operator answered the call, but found no one on the line. As the hotel later explained, that lack of response was "for good reason"—the room from which the call originated had not been refurbished or rented out, so there was no phone in the room!

A telephone in at least one room on the twelfth floor of the Roosevelt has also given the switchboard operators trouble. The particular room is one that famed astrologer and author Linda Goodman rented in 1959 while writing one of her books. During her stay, Goodman indicated that there was "a presence, a special quality" about that room.

According to records at the Hotel Roosevelt, "In October of 1989, that presence made itself known again by telephone." Late one night, Room 1221 lit up on the switchboard. The operator responded, but there was no one on the line. When the light lit up again, the operator double-checked the guest register and found that the room was not occupied. She called Security, explained the situation, and asked that someone check the room and put the phone back on the hook. Security responded, and that was that—until three nights later, when it happened again. This time, the phone got off the hook "by itself" three times in one hour. Each time, Security went up to the room and returned the handset to its cradle; the next time they went up, the phone would again be off the hook.

All of this in an unoccupied, locked room.

As the months went by, more and more floors of the hotel opened up to guests. One day in spring of 1986, Daniel Cichon, Assistant Director of Housekeeping, was giving some of the rooms a final inspection. As he left a suite he'd been inspecting on the eleventh floor, Cichon turned off the lights and locked the door. Moments later, he came back to the rooms, unlocked the door, and was quite startled to find all the lights on.

At about the same time Cichon had his strange experience, Rachel, a lobby maid at the hotel, was restocking her cart with supplies from a storage cupboard. As she reached in to pick out the items she needed, something unseen gave her a firm push into the closet. Assuming that it was just a fellow employee teasing her, Rachel yelled for him to "cut it out." Seconds later, Rachel whirled around to face the prankster—and was horrified to realize that there was no one anywhere near her.

Phantom sounds are also heard in that area of the hotel. The administration reports receiving "calls from guests, late at night, complaining about loud conversations in the next room—but when Security investigates, they find the next room unoccupied." The hotel has also received "calls about people talking loudly in the halls late at night, but Security has never found anyone out there."

More than willing to accept practical explanations for such noises, the management of the hotel acknowledges that "all old buildings creak and moan now and then." However, they also acknowledge that the number of calls they receive about the phantom noises is probably too high for them all to be chalked up to a settling structure—they have received four or five of these calls each month since the hotel reopened.

In November of 1989, a guest called the switchboard to complain about "kids being loud in the room next door." The employee who answered the call assured the guest that there was no one in the next room. "A little later, the same lady called again, this time very insistent that 'those kids are still loud and they *are* next door.'" The switchboard operator dispatched a member of the hotel's security force to investigate. The room was found to be unoccupied.

These sorts of complaints continued for a few years. Some people even mentioned "strange shadows." Neither the noises nor the shadows were ever explained to the satisfaction of ghost enthusiasts.

Two and a half years after the hotel's reopening, an employee named Steve Fava, who was responsible for filling the pop machines in the halls, went about his task. Steve carried a clipboard which held the paperwork for the job. As he moved from floor to floor, stocking the machines, he would put the clipboard on top of the pop dispenser, well within easy reach.

Just as he had the last can of soda loaded into one machine and was ready to head off to fill the next, Steve discovered that his clipboard was no longer where he'd left it. After a thorough search, the puzzled man found his clipboard inside the ice machine, "an arm's length away from the soda machine."

Being a practical sort, Steve "decided he must have put it on the ice machine and [that] it had just slipped off and into the ice." His resolve was somewhat shaken, however, when "on the next floor, it happened again"—and then "on each floor it happened." By the time he reached the 10th floor, Steve was badly shaken and took extra care to be sure to put the clipboard on the soda machine. Once again, he finished stocking the sodas and reached for the clipboard; once again, it was gone. After a great deal of hunting, Steve finally found the clipboard—it was inside the ice machine that time, too.

The rest of the report on that incident indicates that Steve, "his face white with fright, raced to the general manager's office and said, 'Don't ever make me do that again! I swear those machines are haunted.'"

Hotels employ security guards to keep watch over the property. Normally, where surveillance is concerned, the "buck stops" with those employees. At the Hollywood Roosevelt, however, the ghosts keep a watchful eye out for the guards.

In the fall of 1989, several new security guards were hired. One guard, perhaps an especially sensitive person, reported feeling that he was being watched. Upon careful inspection, he determined that no one else was in the area. Even so, he would suddenly feel uncomfortable and would hurry down the hall, hoping to see another person. He never did. Oftentimes it would feel like someone had been standing in the next doorway but had suddenly stepped back inside the room just as he approached. The guard didn't see or hear anything—it was just something that he sensed.

The hotel even has its own "ghost writer." As a release issued by the hotel indicates, "Late one night in September of 1989, the Night Supervisor of Housekeeping was passing the Personnel Office and heard the electric typewriter being used. Knowing that the staff leaves at 5:00 PM, she knocked on the door to see who was in the office. There was no response. Several times she knocked and called out, but there was still no response—only the steady tap-tap-tapping of the typewriter. Next morning, when the personnel staff arrived, the typewriter was still turned on, a chair that had been left at a desk was now arranged in front of the typewriter, and the papers on all of the desks had been neatly arranged."

More recently, Sales Coordinator Karen Bookholt got a real surprise when she entered her own office early one July morning. Her electric typewriter was, as she put it, "typing all by itself." When Karen expressed her alarm, the typing stopped. After taking a deep

During Hollywood's Golden Age, Marilyn Monroe, Montgomery Clift, Betty Grable, Humphrey Bogart and other movie legends were seen in this elegant lobby—and some say they are still present in spirit form.

breath, the woman informed whatever force was at work, "That's okay, you can keep typing." The activity resumed. What a shame that there wasn't any paper in the typewriter either time. A legible message from beyond would certainly have been intriguing!

Ghosts and electrical equipment have often proved to be a volatile combination, and this was certainly the case when a film crew came into the Roosevelt to shoot a documentary about the resident spirits just before Halloween of 1989. Each time the camera operators moved to the corridor outside Room 928, where Montgomery Clift's spirit is thought to be present, lights would inexplicably go out. (Another time, when a crew from the television show *Entertainment Tonight* tried to film a segment in that same room, a camera operator's light actually exploded.) Sound recording equipment broke down while the operators were trying to work on another floor, and when the team moved to the ballroom, the audio equipment was also affected—but only within the cold spot.

At another point in the shoot—and for no reason that anyone could discern—film jammed in the cameras. Perhaps the most interesting moment in the filming ordeal came when the crew set up to capture some footage of a particular mirror—the mirror that had once belonged to Marilyn Monroe. Seconds into shooting the scene, something triggered the alarm in a nearby smoke detector. The crew never did get that shot recorded.

A psychic entering the Roosevelt's Cinegrill room had news for the staff. She announced that she sensed "a very strong presence" in the room. "There's a ghost here," she maintained. "It's a man, a black man—a musician. He plays a clarinet." Prior to the psychic's visit, no one had known of the existence of that particular entity.

The following two incidents, both actual sightings of an apparition, occurred within 48 hours of each other. During the evening of Saturday, December 15, 1990, the Los Angeles County District Attorney's office held their annual holiday dinner and dance in the haunted hotel. As the successful night of celebrating wore down, one of the guests and his wife were enjoying a look at the photographs that adorn the walls of the mezzanine level.

The couple made their way along the display until they came to the area where the mezzanine overlooks the Blossom Room. At that point, they were surprised to hear piano music. Intrigued, the pair followed the sound of the music until they found a piano. Although there was no one playing the instrument, there was a man dressed in a white suit standing beside it. According to hotel records, "the couple spoke to him, but he didn't answer." Then, to add to the couple's confusion, "as they got closer, the man disappeared. He didn't walk away, he vanished!"

When psychic Peter James investigated in March of 1992, he felt the Blossom Room was "clear of ghosts," but "he felt the impressions of people who had been there often in the hotel's early days." Errol Flynn, Betty Grable and Edward Arnold were three of those whose physical presence had left a mark on the psychic atmosphere of the room many years before.

The next sighting was made by an employee the following Monday. Information released by the hotel indicates that the employee involved in this encounter, a man named Billy, is "from the Philippines—a culture that firmly believes in spirits."

Billy was walking along a third floor hallway when he came to a corner. As he looked to his left, he saw a man standing about halfway down the hall. Thinking the man was lost or in need of some kind of assistance, Billy called out to him. The man didn't answer, but because he kept looking from side to side as if he wasn't sure which way to go, the concerned employee approached him. "Billy came closer, within three feet of the man, and again asked if he could be of help. The man still did not reply but turned and walked toward the fire exit at the east end of the hall. Then he walked through the door! He didn't open it and walk out—he went through the door! Billy tried to follow, but his feet were rooted to the spot."

Billy later acknowledged that, while it felt as though he was paralyzed with fear by the experience for five minutes, in reality "it was probably only a few seconds." It would be interesting to arrange a meeting between Billy and the couple who'd seen the manifestation of a man in white standing by the piano. Billy also described the ghost that he saw as wearing a white suit, but that does not necessarily mean it was the same manifestation.

That man in white was probably not the same ghost that a desk clerk saw. According to hotel reports, clerk Troy Robertson was counting his receipts one spring night when "he was startled to see a man walk past him and into the next room. Actually, he was mostly shocked because the man had no face! After a moment of near-panic, Troy cautiously stepped into the doorway to see if there really *was* a man in the room. There was absolutely no one there—and there is no other way in or out of that room." The incident unnerved the employee so badly that he no longer wishes to discuss the experience.

When psychic researcher Peter James investigated the haunted hotel, he had complete cooperation—from both the management of the inn and its ghosts. "At the end of a hallway on the third floor, he received the impression of Carmen Miranda, and near the elevator he felt the presence of Humphrey Bogart. In the Academy Room (which was originally the hotel's library and was used as a meeting place for civic groups and social clubs), Peter encountered the spirit of a little girl—Carol or Caroline—who was looking for her mother. Others had reported seeing a similar ghost, such as the hotel employee who described a "child about five years old, with light brown hair pulled back in a ponytail, wearing a light pink jacket and little blue jeans. She was so cute, skipping around the fountain and singing."

There was an extremely cold spot in the Academy Room which Peter described as a tubular shaft where the spirits enter. This, he felt, was "their gathering place."

The report continued, "In the dark recesses of the old Arthur Murray Dance Studio that adjoins the hotel, Peter felt many spirits, especially on the stairway." More intriguing still is the fact that the stairway in question backs onto an outside wall of the Academy Room—a spot that James had identified as "hiding something valuable of historic significance."

On April 26, 1992, Peter James's camera operator, a man identified only as "Dimtri," filmed the psychic in an amazing battle against an aggressive entity. The entourage was up in the penthouse when Peter "was suddenly grabbed about the legs" by an invisible force. As Peter struggled in vain to free himself and to communicate with the entity, Dimtri continued to let his camera run. The result was a riveting and dramatic clip of film that clearly showed the psychic struggling against an unseen attacker. Through it all, Peter talked to the manifestation and eventually calmed it. The presence, he informed Dimtri, was a former body-guard named Frank. It would seem that the spirit's desire to protect the area did not die with his physical body.

The last place in the hotel that Peter James and his entourage explored was the basement, which he initially declared to be "clean" of ghosts. Seconds later, however, the psychic sensed the spirit of a woman who had once been employed by the hotel. As the entity communicated with Peter, sheets that were hung over a "high rod ... began to undulate." The movement stopped and Peter realized that the spectral presence was no longer in the room. He stepped toward the area where he'd sensed her just a moment before—and found that it was icy cold.

Considering that their grand inn is so thoroughly haunted, it's fortunate that the owners, management and staff of the Hollywood Roosevelt are so wonderfully accepting of their non-paying—and apparently permanent—guests.

Gram's Ghost

The Yucca Valley, east of San Bernadino, is one of the most exotic areas in California. Gnarled and twisted Joshua Trees grow beside dramatically colored piles of rock in the desert, creating a strangely beautiful and decidedly unusual landscape. Perhaps this extraordinary vista has somehow contributed to ufologists' long-cherished theory that there is a secret base for spaceships hidden in the area. Another group believes that the location is a prime spot from which to observe "elementals"—tiny beings whose work supports the natural surroundings. Members of a conference on spiritual development that was held in the Valley some years ago reported both hearing and seeing the diminutive supernatural creatures.

Then there is another group of people who believe that a certain hostelry in the Yucca Valley is very haunted—by the ghost of legendary musician Gram Parsons. Parsons, who almost single-handedly invented the country-rock genre in the '60s and '70s during his tenure with the Byrds and the Flying Burrito Brothers—and who is credited with discovering Emmylou Harris—was only 26 years old when he died of an overdose of morphine and tequila at the Joshua Tree Inn on September 19, 1973. Since his death, the Inn has become an important destination for many fledgling musicians who feel that Gram's spirit lingers there—especially in Rooms 8 and 9.

Evelyn Shirbroun is one of the true believers, which is fortunate because she owns the Joshua Tree Inn. "Yes, I believe," the personable innkeeper began. She went on to explain, "Since we've had it [the Joshua Tree Inn] as a bed and breakfast, the most consistent conversation relates to the moving mirror—the mirror in the bedroom of Room 8 moves for no apparent reason. There was a structural engineer who stayed in there, and he kept saying, 'There's no reason for that mirror to move like that.' He was just beside himself one morning when he came in for breakfast. He had tried everything he could think of to see where the movement was coming from."

Despite his scientific leanings, that engineer was never able to solve the mystery. Perhaps if he'd known that the mirror was the only piece of furniture remaining in the room from the time Gram Parsons had died there, it might have helped to ease the engineer's confusion.

"Most of the guests feel that the moving mirror is caused by Gram," Evelyn explained. The only time an apparition has actually been seen was by a guest in another room. "The guest was a fellow musician," Evelyn said. "He was a pretty straight kid. He reported a presence, a shape, in his room and swore it was Gram Parsons."

Evelyn's most personal proof of the specter came in the days before she opened the inn to the public. She originally bought the place to use it as a retreat for abused children. At that time, she knew nothing about Gram Parsons, much less his ghost.

She did, however, know that "the kids [in her care] used to complain about seeing something or someone in the closet. I didn't know the stories about Gram Parsons's ghost at all, so we started rotating the kids in the rooms."

No matter which children she assigned to which rooms, it was only those kids in Rooms 8 and 9 who were ever bothered by the presence of a ghost.

It was not long before Evelyn met Ben Fong-Torres, a former editor at *Rolling Stone* magazine and author of the book *Hickory Wind: The Life and Times of Gram Parsons*, who told her the whole story. This was knowledge that Evelyn kept to herself. "I could not tell anyone about a ghost being around the grounds, this being a therapeutic milieu for kids," she explained.

Not much later, Evelyn changed the focus of the business to that of a bed and breakfast. From that point on, both the musical disciples and the ghost stories began to flood in.

Although Parsons was a brilliantly talented and creative musician who virtually dedicated his life to his craft, his trailblazing contributions were not widely recognized during his lifetime. Ironically, it was a series of events immediately after his death—and unconnected to the music industry—that introduced the name Gram Parsons to mainstream America.

By 1969, Parsons had ended his tenure with the Byrds and become close friends with Rolling Stone Keith Richards. That unfortunate association started Parsons on a long, sad descent into drug and alcohol abuse. The end began in the third week of September, 1973. Parsons arrived at the Joshua Tree Inn with some friends to begin another of their drug-fueled retreats. What happened from the time of their arrival at the Inn until the last few moments of September 18th, when one of his companions noticed Parsons's labored breathing and phoned for an ambulance, is unknown. All that is known for sure is that Gram Parsons was declared dead of an overdose less than an hour later.

Immediately following Parsons's death, a veritable circus ensued—more than enough commotion to cause any spirit to become restless. Parsons's stepfather claimed the young man's body and arranged to have it shipped east for a funeral. Gram's friends, however, felt that the musician would not have wanted this and, in as bizarre a heist as has ever been executed, they stole the coffin containing Parsons's corpse and took it back to the desert. There, in an attempt at cremation, they set fire to their friend's body. Not surprisingly, the ill-conceived—and illegal—impromptu funeral was soon discovered and charges were laid against Gram's friends. What was left of the musician's charred remains was sent back east to his family.

Evidence of the influence of Gram Parsons as a ghost was probably first seen during the trial against Gram's would-be cremators. The case came to court on November 5, 1973—the date that would have been Gram's 27th birthday. Despite the seriousness of the charges brought against the deceased man's friends, they only received fines and suspended sentences.

Since that time, the site where the men tried to dispose of Parsons's body has become something of a cult shrine for young musicians who wish to honor Gram's memory and his contributions to the world of music—and the Joshua Tree Inn has become a central meeting place for those who hope to commune with Gram's spirit. Psychics who have visited the haunted Rooms 8 and 9 have come away with the definite impression of a spirit. The ghost, presumably Gram himself, creates what those sensitives have described as a "heaviness" in those rooms. It has also been noted that the ghost likes to "borrow" guests' personal possessions such as toiletries and keys.

Despite this, or perhaps because of it, the faithful return again and again, year after year, to haunt the inn that Gram haunts.

Chapter 6
MARINE MANIFESTATIONS

Since the beginning of time, human beings have been drawn to the beautiful, powerful and mysterious sea—yet, if we don't respect its power (and sometimes even when we do), it can easily kill us. This caveat certainly applies to the Pacific Ocean, which is often stormy despite its name. As you might expect, ghostly legends from the sea are plentiful all along the California coastline.

The Haunted Queen

"Most of this generation will be gone, including myself, when this event occurs. However, the *RMS Queen Mary*, launched today, will know its greatest fame and popularity when she never sails another mile and never carries another passenger."

Those eerily prophetic words were spoken by Lady Mabel Fortescue-Harrison as she watched the legendary ocean liner launched from Clydebank, Scotland on September 26, 1934. More than 60 years later, on March 19, 1997, Elizabeth Borsting, then public relations manager for the ship, wrote that "visitors are fascinated with the spirits aboard the haunted *Queen Mary*."

In the years between those two statements, Lady Fortescue-Harrison's prediction has come true, and the British ship that was once called "Queen of the Atlantic" has become a permanent fixture on the shore of the Pacific Ocean in Long Beach, California. The *Queen Mary* has also become one of the world's most haunted vessels.

During its first six years of operation by England's Cunard Line, the opulent and massive ship—1,019.5 feet and 81,237 gross tons compared to the *Titanic*'s 882.9 feet and 46,329 gross tons— ferried royalty, movie stars and business tycoons back and forth across the Atlantic Ocean in grand and glittering style. Four days into the cruise that had begun on August 30, 1939, with $44 million in gold bullion and 2,550 passengers (including Mr. and Mrs. Bob Hope) aboard, the crew was ordered to cover all the ship's portholes. The lives of all on board now depended on the ship remaining undetected. England and France had just declared war against Germany; the icy waters of the Atlantic were full of Nazi warships and U-boats, the skies above crowded with bombers from Hitler's *Luftwaffe*.

The hastily-performed camouflage job foreshadowed the *Queen Mary*'s next incarnation as a troop carrier nicknamed "The Gray Ghost." She was stripped of her luxurious appointments, and her exterior was painted a dull gray color in an apparentl successful attempt to hide the ship from the enemy.

Because the Atlantic crossing was one of the most dangerous wartime maneuvers, the ship's great speed was an important attribute. Unfortunately, it was that lifesaving speed which became directly responsible for a tragic wartime accident—and for the ship becoming incredibly haunted. The *Queen Mary* and her much smaller escort, the *Curacoa*, were sailing together. To make their paths difficult for German submarines to track, both crafts maintained a zigzag pattern. Somehow, a navigational error was made and the huge *Queen Mary* collided with the *Curacoa*, slicing the escort ship in two. Of the 439 crewmen aboard the escort

During WWII, Winston Churchill used the Queen Mary *for dangerous Atlantic crossings. His spirit—along with those of hundreds of phantom wartime sailors—is still thought to be aboard the ship.*

vessel, 338 perished—many by drowning in the freezing water as they watched the larger ship sail away in compliance with strict orders not to stop and rescue those in peril. The trauma was so great that it permanently scarred the ship's atmosphere.

The physical damage to the *Queen Mary* was soon repaired with the application of a 70-ton patch of cement, and she continued in service. Winston Churchill trusted the *Queen Mary* to shuttle him back and forth to North America while the war was at its height. Once peace was declared, the former luxury liner turned troop carrier continued to serve soldiers, but now in a more genteel manner—by making six "bride and baby" crossings, carrying nearly 13,000 war brides and their infants to the United States and Canada. For the next 20 years, the *Queen Mary* again traversed the oceans of the world as a passenger liner, even carrying royalty from time to time.

By December 1967, the *Queen Mary's* days of active service were over. After 1001 transatlantic crossings, she was purchased for $3.45 million and permanently docked by the American city of Long Beach. Her docking was the first step in the fulfillment of Lady Mabel Fortescue-Harrison's prediction some 31 years earlier. From that day forward, the ship that had already served so many different purposes never carried another passenger, never sailed another mile. The *Queen Mary's* register was given to the British Consul General and she was removed from the British Registry of Ships. Now officially classified as a building, the *Queen Mary*, stationary and dependent on shoreside utilities, has realized her greatest fame and popularity as a tourist attraction with hotel, banquet and museum facilities incorporated into her hull.

Shortly after the ship's arrival at her permanent pier, the new owners became all-too-aware that the vessel's varied past had left it extremely haunted. One of the most evident hauntings is in the section of the hull that hit the *Curacoa*. Ship's staff reported that "a television crew left their audio recorder running overnight in the exact location where the two ships collided. As the tape played back the next day, incredible sounds of pounding could be heard. Others have claimed to hear voices and blood-curdling noises from the same area."

Many people have reported hearing the ghostly sounds. Some describe the pounding in the area as a "frantic knocking" or "strange tapping." Others say that they have heard water gushing and metal smashing—the sounds of that fatal accident replaying into eternity. Even more distressing are the phantom shrieks and moans emanating from that area of the ship. The anguished spirits of the sailors who were either killed on impact or left to drown when the two ships collided have become part of the *Queen Mary* herself.

John Smith, who was the *Queen Mary*'s chief engineer when she was retired from service, reported not only hearing tapping but also water rushing into the area that had been damaged by the fatal crash. Smith knew the vessel well, and upon hearing the noises he made an extensive search to locate their source. Despite his skilled efforts, he could find no reasonable explanation for the sounds and concluded that he was hearing ghostly echoes from that horrible tragedy so many years before.

In addition to the psychic damage wrought by the wartime deaths (and a fatal accident during the *Queen Mary*'s initial construction), there have, according to current staff, been 48 "untimely deaths" on board the ship. Many of those spirits have "stayed with the ship."

John Pedder's ghost is one of those spirits. Doorway 13, well below deck, proved to hold the ultimate in bad luck for the young crewman. On July 10, 1966, the 18-year-old was participating in a routine drill. Something went terribly wrong and Pedder was crushed to death instantly. Public Relations Manager Elizabeth Borsting acknowledged that Pedder's manifestation—a bearded young man clad in blue overalls—is frequently seen "walking the length of Shaft Alley … in the depths of the Engine Room."

These reports come from current crew members as well as visitors to the ship-turned hotel and tourist attraction. Nancy Wozny, a former tour guide and security officer with the *Queen Mary*, reported that she felt someone beside her as she was locking up the tour areas one night. "I turned around and saw a man standing behind me," she explained. Although she knew it was always theoretically possible that a visitor could become separated from a tour and left behind, Nancy doubted that this was the case. The image—with its dirty blue overalls, "beautiful beard," "grossly white" skin and complete lack of facial expression—felt all wrong for a tourist. If Nancy suspected she was seeing a ghost, her suspicions were confirmed when the young man simply vanished before her eyes.

The ship's indoor swimming pools still exist, but only for display purposes. They are no longer used—at least not by flesh and blood swimmers. However, two female ghosts continue to take advantage of the first-class aquatic facility. One tour guide had an especially disturbing sighting. She was aware that she was seeing into "another dimension" because, although the manifestation she observed had form enough to reveal that she was wearing a bathing suit, the vision was "in black and white." Seconds later, the strange swimmer disappeared as mysteriously as she had appeared.

One guide reported seeing a woman wearing a vintage 1930s swimsuit, preparing to dive into an almost dry swimming pool. The guide yelled to the woman to stop, then turned around to call security. As she turned back to focus her attention on the apparently insane or suicidal woman, she discovered that the apparition had disappeared.

In 1983, *Queen Mary* employee Lester Hart was on one side of the swimming pool when he saw the image of a blond woman wearing a long-sleeved white gown on the opposite deck. The apparition, which he described as being a "hazy image" (and therefore one he was sure was not a living person), locked onto Hart's gaze.

Hart was understandably shaken by the encounter, but at least it provided a bit of preparation for his next experience. One day while he was working in a shop near the pool, Hart heard water splashing as though someone were swimming. Because a small amount of water is kept in the pool to prevent deterioration, he suspected that a guest had wandered off limits to indulge in an unauthorized dip. Dropping what he had been doing, Hart hurried to the pool. It was deserted—but the water near the pool's ladder was moving, and there were wet footprints leading across the deck toward a doorway.

This seemed to indicate that Hart's initial suspicions about an errant guest had been correct, so he followed the path of footprints assuming they would lead him to the swimmer. His plan was sound, but unfortunately, the wet marks simply stopped as though the feet making them had suddenly vanished. More puzzling still was the fact that the area's highly-sensitive alarm system was on but had not been triggered by any motion in the vicinity of the pool.

Hart now knew that he had experienced an encounter with one of the swimming pool ghosts, presumably the one who's been seen wearing a 1930s-era swimsuit. Another spirit is known to haunt that area, but is usually dressed in street clothes that witnesses identify as being from the 1960s.

There is at least one more ghost in the pool area. This one usually manifests only as the sound of childish laughter, but occasionally the image of a forlorn little boy has been seen. The lad might not be so sad if he knew that he could find ghostly playmates on board. In an area of the ship that was once a playroom but is now used for storage, many people have heard the sounds of children playing. An infant who died just hours after being born can also still be heard crying.

The most imposing ghost aboard the luxurious ship/hotel is that of none other than Winston Churchill. Although his spirit is not a constant presence, echoes of his famous cigars still linger in the stateroom that was once his. The distinctive smoke can be seen and smelled quite clearly on occasion; the phantom traces are very localized and cannot be attributed to the smoking habits of anyone on board at the time—well, not anyone still living.

Churchill's former cabin is not the only one haunted. The ghost of a purser who was murdered during an attempted robbery has rendered Room B-340 too haunted to be rented out. The administration assumes that few hotel guests would willingly endure having to dodge objects flying around the room, listening to drawers rattling, trying to sleep while their bed is shaking, or being grabbed at by unseen hands.

There have, however, been reports of ghostly activity in several other first class staterooms. According to the ship's administration, "there have been reports of water running in the middle of the night, phones ringing at early hours of the morning and lights suddenly turning on in the middle of the night. Passengers have reported hearing heavy breathing and feeling people tugging at their covers, only to realize that there was no one in the room with them."

The ghost in the ship's kitchen area is the disembodied spirit of a murdered man. Not surprisingly, it is an extremely angry and restless soul. The haunting dates back to an event during the ship's wartime service as "The Gray Ghost," when an enlisted man reportedly attacked a cook. The skirmish quickly became ugly and the victim was thrown into a hot stove. The wronged man's spirit still flings dishes around the kitchen and cries out against the injustice brought upon him. He also causes the lights to go on and off when no one can be seen near the switches, and he will periodically make off with a commonly used kitchen utensil, only to return it later when no one's looking for it.

Not all of the *Queen Mary*'s ghosts are former humans. The barking of a dog, thought to be the ghost of an Irish setter, still resonates through one area of the ship while the animal eternally frets about his owner. Pets were allowed on the ship when the *Queen Mary* was a luxury liner but, unless you could afford VIP status, any animal with which you were traveling had to be housed in one of the kennels on the sundeck. An Englishman who sailed frequently always brought his beloved Irish Setter with him. The dog was a well-trained and highly obedient animal who enjoyed his walks around the ship with his owner, but also accepted that after those outings he would once again be locked into his kennel.

Because this routine had long been established, the crew was quite surprised when the dog, apparently unprovoked, began to howl and to paw at the cage door as though trying to escape. The person in charge of the area opened the distraught animal's cubicle to see what was wrong. The dog appeared to be all right physically, but judging by the animal's frantic circles around the kennel area, he was extremely agitated about something.

Not knowing what else to do, the kennel supervisor sent a messenger to the owner's cabin, thinking that perhaps the master could settle his pet down. Sadly, this was not to be the case—the man lay dead in his bed. The dog's strange behavior was seemingly its reaction to the death of his beloved friend and owner.

The poor animal was so inconsolable that his mournful howling can still be heard. Many people have tried to follow the sounds to their source, but no matter how close they think they're getting to it, the ghostly baying still seems to be coming from far away.

Senior Second Officer William Stark's ghost is easier to pin down because his image is actually seen wandering about the enormous ship. The man died on board the *Queen Mary* in September 1949 as a direct result of his drinking problem. While drunk, he mistakenly consumed a bottle of tetrachloride and died almost immediately. Perhaps because he had no idea that his last cocktail was a lethal one, Stark's confused but harmless soul has remained aboard the *Queen Mary*.

Another ghostly sailor, wearing his white dress uniform and proudly displaying his ribbons, has also been seen. When he is spotted, witnesses report that the image is distinct but completely transparent.

Another phantom haunts the room that was originally the Main Lounge and is now known as the Queen's Salon. According to present-day staff, "a beautiful woman clad in a simple white evening gown is often seen dancing alone in the shadows. One unsuspecting little girl pointed the 'woman in white' out to her tour guide. The guide looked over and saw nothing, but the little girl described the woman in quite some detail. Still, the guide saw nothing and continued with the tour. The child continued to repeat her observation, not knowing that she was just one in a long list of visitors who had seen this mysterious woman."

An area of the *Queen Mary* called the Pig 'n' Whistle has been done up to resemble an English pub. Whatever spirit haunts this room is not always present—but when it is, *everyone* is aware of it. Plates fly off the wall one after another; pictures, and even a clock on the wall, have been found hanging upside down.

People have also glimpsed a specter in white overalls that is apparently still working in areas that were once engine rooms. It is presumed that he is a revenant from the ship's earliest days. Another entity, who also seems to know his way around the below-deck area, is invisible but manages to make the chains at the side of a passageway sway as though someone had run along the corridor with their hand on the chain.

The ghost of a well-dressed man haunts an area near the first-class suites. He has dark hair and is wearing a suit that witnesses judge to be from the 1930s. A photographer might actually have inadvertently snapped the ghost's picture. According to hotel administration, "a tour guide was taking interior photographs. One picture, which captured the cabin's beautiful tinted mirror, was taken from across the room. When the photos were developed, the particular print featured the reflection of a tall, dark-haired man in the mirror. This would not be considered unusual except for the fact that the man in the photo was wearing a 1930s-style suite and did not resemble the tour guide in the least." In closing, the writer noted that at the time the strange picture was taken "the tour guide was alone."

No one knows which of the many ghosts on the *Queen Mary* is responsible for turning lights on and off, for unlocking locked doors and, in some cases, even propping those doors open. It could be the specter who turned skeptical local reporter Tom Hennessy into a believer.

In March of 1983, Hennessy spent a night alone aboard the ship—a night he'll never forget. By prior agreement, the scribe was left in some of the most haunted areas of the *Queen Mary* for prearranged lengths of time. He was "serving his time"—all 35 minutes of it—in Shaft Alley when something supernatural joined him. Just as he was settling in at the undeniably unappealing spot, he began to hear the ghostly banging that he had been told so much about. Hennessy bravely made his way toward the noise, but just as he came near it, the banging stopped. He turned around to go back to where he'd been; unfortunately, although he was locked in and completely alone in the engine area, his path was now blocked by an enormous oil drum. He turned around and went the other way, but he knew he'd eventually have to get back to his original perch, so he tried again. This time his way was blocked by not one but two oil drums. Worse, he could feel the catwalk beneath his feet shaking as though someone was walking toward him. Understandably, Hennessy hurried away from the approaching rumble.

Not long after Hennessy had calmed himself from that encounter, the poor beleaguered reporter had an even more disturbing experience when he suddenly realized he was overhearing a conversation from somewhere in the vicinity. The voices he heard were distinct enough that he was certain there were three men talking. The trio of voices soon reduced itself to only one, but that single psychic echo was so distinct that Hennessy was able to make out the words: "I'm turning the lights off." Fortunately, the terrified reporter was let out of Shaft Alley before being thrust into darkness.

Tom Hennessy left the *Queen Mary* a changed man, and from what I've been able to find out, he has never again attempted to stay alone in the place. That's not to say that he hasn't been back.

The spectacular Queen Mary *was once called "Queen of the Atlantic." She is now permanently docked in Long Beach and open to visitors—including ghost hunters.*

Thousands and thousands of people visit the haunted *Queen Mary* every year; many come hoping to see at least one of the ghosts—and many do.

As a postscript, Lady Mabel Fortescue-Harrison, who died in Hollywood in the mid-1950s, was absolutely right. The *Queen Mary* definitely gained "its greatest fame and popularity" *after* the grand vessel was docked permanently. Lady Mabel's prediction must have seemed bizarre when she made it, but those prophetic words actually served to seal her place in history.

Hornet—Nest for Phantoms

Like the *Queen Mary*, the *USS Hornet* has a proud history of service and is now permanently docked. And, like the *Queen Mary*, the *Hornet* is also very haunted.

Stationed at Alameda Point near San Francisco, the aircraft carrier is open to the public as a museum. Staff and volunteers are all people who are experienced with and comfortable on the vessel. They're also not the kinds of people who are prone to wild flights of fantasy. Yet many of them acknowledge having had paranormal encounters while on board. The *Hornet's* marketing manager, for example, watched in amazement as an apparition dressed in officer's khakis made his way toward the engine room—and then simply vanished.

According to workers' reports, ghosts seem to be constantly watching over them as they work. There were many witnesses when, a few Decembers ago, the ghost of a sailor ran along the hangar deck and disappeared right into a Christmas tree. A thorough search of the premises determined that there was absolutely no one aboard who shouldn't have been—no one who was still alive, that is.

Other presences on the *Hornet* are only heard, not seen. After listening to footsteps nearby, people reasonably expect to find a flesh and blood person making the sounds. On the *Hornet*, this is often not the case. Spookier still are the conversations that are frequently overheard—conversations from years ago which sometimes replay themselves for today's listeners. Like many of the ghostly images that are seen, these voices may simply be the result of energy recorded in the environment—echoes that provide witnesses with a glimpse into yesterday. Many of these manifestations seem completely unaware of the existence of today's world around them. Others, like the officer wearing his dress uniform and making his way to the pilot house, make eye contact with the living. Even so, it's difficult to guess whether or not any of the ghosts are aware of the presence of corporeal beings.

All those who have sensed the phantom presences aboard the *USS Hornet* agree that the spirits are helpful ones who must have had some sort of an association with the ship in life and want her to have a successful "afterlife."

The Occidental Ghost

Sailors have always shared something of a loose-knit, informal feeling of community with one another. For this reason, sea-faring men all over the world had been aware of the entity aboard a ship christened the *Occidental* since the ghost's initial appearance in 1887. It wasn't until some years later, however, that ordinary citizens became aware of the phenomenon when an article about the haunted ship appeared in the newspaper *The Hawaiian Star*.

The brief article explained that sailors aboard the ship saw "the ghost of Captain Williams frequently and give a perfect description of the dead man." The article went on to say that the ghost usually "looked ahead intently for several seconds, turned, as if to give orders, uttered a short agonizing groan, staggered amidships and disappeared."

That ghostly scenario was an exact reenactment of Williams's murder during a mutiny aboard the *Occidental* in the spring of 1887.

Despite the superstitions sailors generally have about being aboard a haunted ship, the *Occidental*—complete with the dead captain's apparition—continued to roam the seas well into the 1890s.

Murder So Foul

The year was 1890. The ship, a Norwegian craft named the *Squando*, was docked at San Francisco when her captain discovered that his wife had been unfaithful to him. Worse, the woman's lover was the ship's first mate. Although the names of those involved in the tragic ocean-going triangle have been lost to time, their actions have left a permanent legacy.

Once she realized that her unfaithful act had been found out, the captain's wife immediately rediscovered her long-lost respect for her wedding vows—and together the devious married couple plotted the indiscreet sailor's murder. She coaxed the unsuspecting first mate into drinking far more than was good for him. As soon as he was too intoxicated to defend himself, the woman held her former lover still while her husband swung an ax across his neck. Seconds later they threw his body—and then his head—overboard.

The following morning, the murderers were in for an unpleasant surprise; the headless corpse had surfaced and was floating in plain sight through the waters of San Francisco Bay. The couple fled the ship in terror. This left the *Squando* without either a captain or a first mate. Although no record exists of the captain and his wife ever being brought to justice for their terrible deed, we do know that the company that owned the *Squando* kept the vessel in service. At least tried to.

The next three captains hired by the shipping company were all killed while on board the *Squando*. The ship developed a well-deserved reputation for being either jinxed or haunted—or both. In 1893, while the *Squando* was docked in Eastern Canada, the entire crew abandoned the ship. Word spread throughout the shipping community, and the ill-fated vessel's owner soon found that no sailor in the world would sign on for duty aboard the cursed vessel. The owners had little choice but to leave her docked where she was.

To prevent looting, the company hired local men to guard the ship. Within a few shifts, each one of a succession of guards had deserted the craft. Not one of them ever worked a moment beyond the time they saw the bloody, headless apparition lurking in the dark hallway by the captain's quarters.

The owners may not have believed the wild tales they were hearing about their ship, but they did know that a commercial craft that could be neither manned nor guarded served no purpose whatsoever. No doubt thinking they were putting an expensive but necessary end to the horror of the *Squando*, the Norwegian company ordered her torn apart and sold for salvage. Apparently their solution was not an entirely successful one; some years later, witnesses standing on San Francisco's SkyDeck Observatory at Embarcadero Center described a ship they had seen sailing out from a fog bank—a ship meeting the exact description of the long-destroyed *Squando*. Her demolition had seemingly only changed her from a ship of the physical world to a phantom ship from another dimension.

Ghostly Lifesaver

Despite its often pleasant climate, rolling hills and spectacular bay views, San Francisco is not a good place to be down on your luck. Unfortunately, that is exactly the situation in which two young men, Eric and Peter, found themselves at some point during the mid-1950s. By the time they met up with the captain of a tramp steamer, the two men were broke, hungry and, in a word, desperate—desperate enough to accept the captain's offer of work that was described to them as being "legal but dangerous."

Eric and Peter were aboard the steamer and a good five days sail from San Francisco when, in the middle of the night, a vicious fire broke out aboard. Angry-looking flames soon engulfed the entire vessel, leaving the crew no alternative but to don lifejackets and plunge into the sea. By the time the first thin light of dawn crested the horizon, the ship was gone. Eric and Peter were both still alive, but just barely. The two men were totally exhausted, too tired to do anything but simply float and wait for death to claim them as she had claimed the crewmates whose bodies bobbed lifelessly around them in the water.

The two were so resigned to the inevitability of their fate that, when Peter first saw an apparent mirage, he was sure it was a near-death hallucination. *No one* could be out rowing a small craft in the middle of the Pacific Ocean. And yet, that is precisely what he thought he saw. Surely, Peter mused, it was his fast-approaching death from dehydration that caused the image to appear in his mind's eye. He was confused, therefore, when he saw Eric staring intently in the same direction—apparently at the same image which Peter had been certain was merely a figment of his own demented imagination.

Neither Eric nor Peter could believe their ears when, moments later, the man in the tiny craft began to speak to them. The man explained that he was the sole survivor of a ship that had gone down in the area. Peter refused to waste what little energy he had left by trying to communicate with an illusion, but Eric struggled to ask the man if he had any food or drink that he would be willing to share. As if in reply, the strange man at the oars reached into the water and pulled out a good-sized fish, which he immediately proceeded to break in half. As he handed one half to Eric and the other to Peter, he told them, "Drink the water from its innards and then chew on its flesh for sustenance."

The young men did as they were instructed. The nourishment restored their strength sufficiently to climb into the rowboat with the man. Peter and Eric tried to thank their rescuer, but he seemed to have become disoriented and kept berating himself for having been a fool.

The motley trio spent the entire day crowded into the small craft and floating in the middle of the Pacific Ocean. By dusk they were able row toward a deserted island, where they spent the night.

When the first light of dawn woke the young men the next morning, they were surprised to see that their Good Samaritan was preparing to leave in his little boat. Before he rowed off, however, he asked the stranded young men if they would do a favor for him. Without consulting one another, both Eric and Peter eagerly agreed to help the kind man who had saved their lives.

"I'm going to tell you my wife's address, and also the number for a safety deposit box in San Francisco," he explained. "The key for the box is in the shed behind my wife's house. I want my wife to have everything that is in that box."

"But, what if we're not rescued?" Eric asked.

"You will be," the man assured the pair. As he rowed away from Eric and Peter he called out, "You'll be safely back in San Francisco in just a few days."

With their companion gone, both men's hearts sank. Eric and Peter lay on the shore of a tiny island that was not much more than an outcropping of rock. Once again the young men were sure that they would soon be dead. Just when their spirits were at lowest ebb, fate seemed to deal them an even more crushing blow. An airplane flew low overhead, tantalizing them with the realization that, while they had little chance of being rescued, they were apparently not many miles from civilization. As the two watched in amazement, the plane's cargo hold opened up and a parcel was tossed out.

Eric reached the package first.

"Look!" he cried, tearing open the lifesaving pack of supplies. Inside was something even more important than the much needed food and water—a three-word message reading, "Ship On Way." Early the next morning, the two young men who'd given themselves up for dead twice in the space of just a few days watched in wide-eyed wonder as a ship steamed toward them.

Once they were safely on board the Coast Guard rescue vessel, both Eric and Peter asked how they had come to be found. While he was giving them blankets and hot drinks, a sailor explained that a man in a rowboat had advised the Coast Guard of the stranded men's position. Although they were thoroughly confused by all that had happened, Peter and Eric were also extremely relieved, so they settled in to enjoy the sail back to port.

When they'd recovered sufficiently from their grueling experience, Eric and Peter set about making good on their promise to the man in the rowboat. As soon as they had located the correct address, they went to see their rescuer's wife. The woman greeted the young men with mild amusement but did allow that, yes, there was a shed in her backyard and, yes, they were more than free to inspect it if doing so would make them happy.

Moments later, she was astonished to see that the two strangers were handing her a key and delivering a message: "Your husband said that this key will fit a safety deposit box at your bank." They then repeated the box number that the man in the rowboat had given them.

The woman became nearly hysterical at the news. She told Eric and Peter that their information could not possibly be correct—her husband had been dead for eight years. He had died after falling overboard from the deck of a cargo ship sailing out of San Francisco, and his body had never been recovered. All three now realized that the young sailors had been rescued by a ghost—a ghost who then used the lads as messengers to get specific information to his widow. The sailor's wife later opened the safety deposit box and found it full of cash.

Checks into marine accidents off the coast of San Francisco during 1948 bear out this fantastic story. Records show that, during a vicious storm, the captain of a large sailing vessel ordered his crew to come on deck. Unfortunately, one of those sailors—a man matching the description of the mysterious apparition who'd rescued Eric and Peter—was drunk. In his confused state, the man failed to understand that a hurricane was approaching. He climbed into a small rowboat and lowered it into the turbulent ocean. Perhaps the poor man was somehow hoping to flee from the danger.

Neither the tiny, inadequate craft nor the drunken sailor manning its oars were ever seen alive again.

Father Returns

A glorious Fourth of July was especially sweet for one Los Angeles family in 1959. As a special treat to celebrate the holiday, Maria Hernandez had taken her three children to Laguna Beach. Jesus, her only son, was eight years old; her two daughters were a few years younger. Maria was a widow whose husband had been killed in an accident at work two years earlier.

As she played in the sand with her two little girls, Maria kept a close eye on Jesus, who was just a few feet in front of them, running his toy truck along the beach. She turned her attention back to her daughters for just a moment before scanning back to check on her son again. But he wasn't there! In that brief instant, Jesus had disappeared.

Maria began screaming for the lifeguards to find her son. Within seconds, the rescuers had organized the people on the beach into a human chain. They were determined to find the little boy immediately, because if they allowed even an extra minute to go by, Jesus could be swept out of reach by the powerful ocean currents. The search party moved as quickly as they dared while the mother and her two daughters huddled together in fear.

Suddenly a man came running toward the hastily assembled group of lifesavers. He was yelling that a man had brought a little boy ashore just a few yards down the beach. Maria and her daughters raced to the spot the man was indicating. There, alone and shivering on a rock, was Jesus.

"Where's the man who saved you?" Maria asked, hugging the little boy tightly to her breast. "I must thank him."

"It was Papa," the boy replied. Jesus went on to explain that he'd been swept out too far and had started to panic when his father had suddenly appeared in the water. "He helped me swim to shore, then he went back to heaven."

By this time, a crowd had gathered. They smiled when they heard the boy's story because they could see that there was no man nearby who could have rescued him. The boy must have been knocked out cold and dreamed the rescue as he was washed back to shore, they reasoned.

But the man who'd watched Jesus being carried onto the beach did not smile. He knew that the boy was telling the truth. He pointed to a set of fresh footsteps on the beach—they came out of the water, stopped at the rock where Jesus sat, and then continued off into the distance. The man followed those markings and was amazed when, some 50 feet down the beach, they abruptly ended—as though the person who made them had simply vanished into thin air.

When he returned to the spot where the Hernandez family remained huddled around the rock, the man described the person he'd seen carrying Jesus out of the water. The description matched that of Maria's late husband in every detail. Evidently, the dead man's soul had returned in a physical form just long enough to save his son.

Swimming Into Eternity

An actual sighting of a ghost is a rarity. It is far more common to hear reports of people "sensing a presence" when they appear to be alone, or of finding traces of a ghost's movements by noting objects which have mysteriously changed location. A photograph of a ghost is even more unusual, but some do exist. One of the earliest examples of a spirit image being captured on film consists of a single photo in a series of eight shots.

The poignant story behind those pictures begins aboard the *Waterton*, an American tanker owned by an oil company known as Cities Service. The ship was sailing to Panama from California on what should have been a routine journey. Many of the crew members were no doubt especially grateful to be employed because this was December 1929—the New York Stock Exchange had just crashed and the Great Depression had begun.

Tragically, two of the sailors aboard the *Waterton* died during the voyage. James Courtney and Michael Meehan were asphyxiated by fumes that had collected while they were working below deck. Following a solemn service organized by Captain Keith Tracy, the other sailors bid goodbye to their fallen comrades. Weights were attached to the corpses and the dead men were buried at sea.

The deceased were clearly unready to accept their fate, because they were back among their shipmates the very next day. The captain, routinely scanning the horizon with binoculars, was the first to spot the men—swimming along with apparent ease in the middle of the turbulent ocean. He ordered engine adjustments so that the *Waterton* could be brought closer to the swimmers.

By the time the vessel was maneuvered close to the spot the captain had identified, many of those aboard had seen the amazing sight. There were Courtney and Meehan, readily recognizable as sailors they'd buried at sea less than 24 hours before, seemingly unaware of the fact that they were dead.

As the ship inched closer to the miraculous spectacle, the swimmers vanished in the vast expanse of water that was their graveyard—only to instantly reappear a short distance away. The crew was understandably startled by the paranormal event they were witnessing, but after a while it became evident that the swimmers from beyond meant no harm, and the normal routine aboard the *Waterton* resumed.

The ghosts of Michael Meehan and James Courtney swam effortlessly alongside their ship for three days. They stayed the course with great consistency, except to swim ahead once in an apparent attempt to divert the *Waterton*, a warning that saved the ship from being battered by a severe squall ahead.

Upon reaching land, the ship's captain reported the deaths and the strange sightings to his employer. Cities Service Company wasn't about to readily accept this story, even though the officer provided sworn statements from all of his men. Instead, just before his next voyage, the captain was given a camera and told to produce photographs of the phantom swimmers.

As the ship made its way to the coordinates where the crew had last seen their dead compatriots, deckhands and officers alike began to search the seemingly vacant waves of the Pacific Ocean. At twilight, one of the men thought he spotted a pair of figures trailing the ship's wake, but in the lessening light it was impossible to say for certain. As dawn broke the next morning, the crew once again checked aft of the vessel. Nothing. Perhaps the hopeful sailor's enthusiasm of the night before had not been warranted.

Then a deckhand called out to the captain from further toward the bow. There, once again swimming alongside the *Waterton*, were Meehan and Courtney. The captain quickly began to snap photos. He was able to take a series of eight pictures before the ghosts vanished into the deep.

Now armed with photographic proof, the entire crew was impatient to return to port. This time, no one could look at them askance when they spoke of the spectral swimmers they'd seen. Upon landing, the captain immediately took the exposed film to be developed. Not trusting anyone to give sufficient care to his carefully recorded proof, the anxious man stayed in the film laboratory while the negatives were processed.

The captain stood and stared in total disbelief as first one, then a second, and then a third negative appeared before his eyes—each devoid of any images except for the gently rolling waves of the Pacific Ocean. He was devastated. There were seven frames processed now, and none showed what he and his men had seen so clearly. Finally, on the eighth frame, the captain's sanity and that of his crew was vindicated—the eighth shot showed two objects in the ocean, not far from where the photographer had been standing.

As quickly as possible, the developer processed that eighth negative one step further. Once it had been made into an actual print, the images of the two ghost swimmers in the photograph were readily apparent. Everyone who had known Michael Meehan and James Courtney recognized them as soon as they were shown the picture.

Cities Service has long ago ceased to be an active corporation. Their company records, however, are likely stored somewhere. Perhaps still remaining among those records is a photograph of two swimming specters.

Phantoms of the Pacific

A ghost ship is one of the eeriest of all paranormal phenomena. Sailors have reported seeing specific ships, and even hearing the officers on board bark orders at the crew, only to discover that the particular boat they've been observing sunk some time before. Some phantom ships are seen only once, while others repeatedly appear in one particular area. These mysterious vessels from beyond the veil appear all around the world—including the waters of the Pacific Ocean off the California coast. The following tale is especially intriguing because it indicates that, while they can be seen by the human eye, the ghostly craft cannot be detected by radar.

World War II was at its bloody height when, on a cold and foggy night in December of 1942, the *USS Kennison* was making its way toward San Francisco. On the deck, enlisted man Jack Cornelius strained his eyes in a vain attempt to penetrate the fog bank. When the sailor thought he saw a change in the dense blanket surrounding his ship, he stared even more intently. Was the fog thickening? No, not at all. Something was coming through the misty curtain and into view.

For a moment Cornelius, couldn't believe his eyes. In a near panic, he shouted to the man on watch to look at the strange sight approaching their ship. It was a two-masted clipper or, more precisely, the ghost of one. The two men stared at the ancient vessel in fascinated horror. As the manifestation came closer, the men could hear its timbers creaking and the waves slapping against its hull. Fearing they were about to be involved in a collision, the pair spread an alarm throughout the *Kennison*. Moments later, the strange image melted back into the fog and disappeared.

When Cornelius and his fellow witness checked with the sailor manning the radar post, they were told in no uncertain terms that the ship's finely-honed instruments had not registered *anything* in their vicinity for many miles. Once safely back in port, they continued their investigation in vain. The men eventually came to realize that they had simply joined the ranks of seamen who'd seen one of the otherworldly derelict ships that occasionally sail through the curtain of time.

Buildings Haunted by Sailors

As the following stories illustrate, not all the ghosts of old salts are able to find, or are even interested in finding, their old vessels.

People who have devoted much of their lives to the sea are a unique and dedicated group. Some are so dedicated that they seem unable to leave their earthly posts. The Point Vicente Lighthouse, in the Ranchos Palos Verdes area of Los Angeles, seemed unoccupied by ethereal beings until authorities covered over the windows that face away from the sea. Strange as it may seem, that pragmatic act, made out of consideration for nearby residents, coincided with the first signs of a haunting.

Local experts surmise that the tall female ghost who is routinely seen walking around the base of the tower is the spirit of the first lighthouse keeper's wife.

Further south, near San Diego, both the Point Loma Lighthouse and San Miguel Island are haunted by an especially enduring

Gloomy stretches of California coastline are often home to seashore spec-ters—such as the ghosts thought to haunt the Point Vicente and Point Loma lighthouses.

ghost. In 1542, long before anything resembling a lighthouse existed on the point, Juan Rodriguez Cabrillo claimed the area for Portugal. Some who've heard the ghostly moaning and dis-embodied footsteps that reverberate through the abandoned lighthouse believe that the explorer's spirit has never left the land.

Cabrillo died while exploring San Miguel Island, so his mis-sion was never completed. His soul may have returned after death to complete what he wasn't able to finish in life. If so, he's not alone in the area's ghostly realm, although it's unlikely he would approve of his ethereal companions—the place is also haunted by the ghosts of two bohemian commune leaders who committed suicide rather than surrender themselves or their land.

Shoreline Specters

Beautiful Lake Tahoe is located in north central California, about as far east as you can go and still be in the state. On the south shore of the lake, tucked into Emerald Bay, is a strangely haunted island. The ghost is thought to be that of Dick Barter, who arrived in the area in 1863. Barter was a sailor who only intended to pass through the area on his way to the coast. Unfortunately, he took his small boat out on the waters of Lake Tahoe just before a January storm. He was in need of provisions but never made it to his destination of Rowland's Station. He did make it back to shore two days later, but by then much of his body was frozen. His toes eventually succumbed to gangrene.

That brush with mortality had a profound effect on the man's mental stability, and he was never able to complete his journey to the coast. Instead, he settled in the Tahoe area and became a source of endless curiosity for those around him. Among other things, Barter built his own tomb and left detailed instructions about his burial.

Unfortunately, he died in a boating accident and his body was never recovered; no one was ever able to carry out his wishes. Judging by the high levels of ghostly activity in the area, Barter's dream has still come true in a way—those who know the story are certain that his spirit continues to haunt the empty tomb he built.

In the late 1800s, a prosperous fishing community existed south of San Francisco on Santa Cruz Island. The residents were entrepreneurs who caught abalone and shipped it to Asia, where it was in great demand for its supposedly life-enhancing properties. One worker harvesting the fish accidentally jammed his hand between two rocks. The boulders held fast and the man was caught, unable to move. Legend has it that he screamed for help until he was too weak to scream any longer. If anyone heard his cries for help, no one came to his rescue. Determined not to die on the shore when the tide came in, the man did the only thing he could under the circumstances—he took out his knife and began to use his free hand to sever the one that was wedged between the rocks.

Predictably, the worker bled to death before he could finish the gruesome task. His restless spirit, still wearing a distinctive wide-brimmed hat, is reportedly seen along the rocky shore even today.

Yachting with the Duke

In the spring of 1979, a lawyer named Lynn Hutchins purchased a yacht named *The Wild Goose*. Hutchins knew that the sale of the yacht had been heart-rending for its owner, actor John Wayne. The Duke was a man famous for not showing his emotions. At the time of the transaction, Wayne was dying; it was important for him to find the most suitable new owner for his beloved craft. For this reason, the lawyer was especially proud to have been able to purchase the famous yacht and determined right from the outset that he'd keep it as he found it, going so far as to hire the same crew and to preserve Wayne's personal library and trophy wall. Right up to the time of his death on June 11, John Wayne continued to be content in the knowledge that *The Wild Goose* would be well cared for.

Not long after Hutchins took possession of the vessel, he was browsing in a store that specialized in marine accessories. Suddenly and unexpectedly, he felt strongly compelled to buy a particular set of lamps. Puzzled at what he suspected was merely an uncharacteristic occurrence of impulse shopping, Lynn Hutchins returned to the yacht and hung the fixtures in place without mentioning the incident to anyone.

When a long-standing crew member saw the lamps, he was enormously surprised. They were identical to lamps that had hung in *The Wild Goose* for years, and which had only been taken down because the six-foot, four-inch John Wayne kept bumping his head into them. By coincidence, Hutchins had even hung the fixtures in exactly the same spots.

"The man's getting me to do his shopping for him," Hutchins quipped. And apparently his interior decorating as well.

The first actual ghost sighting occurred at 4:00 one morning, just outside the boat's bathroom—or "head," as it is called in nautical lingo. The image was so vivid that Hutchins thought there really was someone on board until he approached the image and watched it disappear without a trace.

Given Hutchins's description of what he had seen, it *had* to be the ghost of John Wayne. The lawyer described a "big, tall figure" that "filled the whole doorway" and wore a cowboy hat. The apparition offered "a bit of a smile" before disappearing from view. Hutchins's wife, Cynde, has also seen what she believes to be the ghost of the late actor on *The Wild Goose*. While enjoying what used to be Wayne's private shower, she sensed that someone was staring at her. The pretty young woman cut her bathing routine short and rather self-consciously got out of the cubicle with a towel in front of her. Virtually filling the doorway to the room was a large form. As she stared at the image, it vanished, taking with it her uncomfortable feeling of being watched.

Neither Hutchins's experience nor his wife's were on the lawyer's mind one afternoon in October of 1979 as he sat relaxing in the yacht's main salon. When he heard clinking sounds coming from the bar across the room, Hutchins got up to investigate and glanced into a mirror hanging above the bar just in time to see a tall man in cowboy attire standing directly behind the chair that Hutchins had just left. Again, the image was so sharp and solid that it fooled the boat's new owner. He thought he had a stowaway until the figure disappeared once again.

Hutchins now says that he never feels as safe anywhere as he does when he's on board *The Wild Goose*. He feels certain that the former owner's spirit is a protective one and that neither man wants any harm to come to the boat. Hutchins has come to believe that the rhythmic thumping he hears on the deck every night is Wayne maintaining his habit of walking 20 laps around the ship. Given the actor's size, one wouldn't expect him to walk silently; apparently his ghost doesn't, either. Others, even those without a vested interest in *The Wild Goose*, have also reported hearing the heavy footsteps on the deck.

A dramatic incident in 1980 confirmed the ghost's protective nature. A wedding was being held on board the yacht as it rode, under its own power, among the other ships in Newport Harbor—close to the property where *The Wild Goose*'s famous former owner had lived. In what was probably a simple crew error, the yacht's engines suddenly stopped without warning. The boat sat powerless in the crowded harbor. Without the engines functioning, there was no way to control the ship; an uncontrolled ship in an enclosed and crowded body of water was an accident waiting to happen. Worse, it takes several minutes to restart the engines once they go dead.

To the complete amazement of all those aboard, *The Wild Goose* did not float about aimlessly while the crew was working to return the ship's power—far from it! Instead, the yacht moved in a controlled manner—against the force of a 40-knot wind—and came to rest gently in the soft mud at the shore in front of John Wayne's former home. It doesn't take much of a stretch of the imagination to conclude that the craft's previous owner had taken over the controls during the emergency.

After Lynn Hutchins had owned the yacht for a number of years and was completely comfortable with the actor's continuing ghostly presence, he invited a group of psychics on board the 140-foot yacht. After exploring the craft, they brought back even more information than Hutchins had expected. One member of the group, Janice Hayes, reported receiving strongly negative vibrations while in the crew area below deck. She determined that there had been controversy surrounding a young crew member who'd shown too much of an independent streak for his own good.

The ship's records confirmed her feelings; 20 years earlier, two young deckhands and a third young man defied direct orders by taking a small boat out while *The Wild Goose* was anchored in choppy waters. The trip proved to be just as dangerous as had been anticipated and resulted in both crew members drowning.

Hutchins was certainly not surprised when the group identified the hallway leading to the head as a "hot spot," because this was where he had first encountered the actor's ghostly manifestation. One of the psychic investigators even reported receiving an expression of love from John Wayne for his longtime friend Patricia Stacey.

The psychics also determined that the boat was still home to a former crew member, probably a man named Peter Stein. Stein served as captain of the ship until his death in 1969 and was a stereotypically colorful sort of old salt whose company John Wayne had always thoroughly enjoyed.

Because these presences have always given the impression of benevolence, it is easy to see why *The Wild Goose*'s owner, Lynn Hutchins, feels very much at home aboard his enormous haunted yacht.

Chapter 7
STAGE FRIGHT

Actors, and the crews that support their theatrical efforts, tend to be a devoted, dedicated and highly emotional group of individuals. The actor's job is an odd one at best: In an artificial setting, with the help of other theater staff, he or she works to convince another group of individuals—the audience—that the fictional is factual. Performers and audiences alike enter into a pact to "willingly suspend their disbelief." Judging by the number of haunted theaters in the world, this kind of environment is apparently conducive to phantom visitations. Perhaps this helps to explain why there is something inherently eerie about an empty theater.

Although I'd certainly never argue against the premise that many theaters are homes to ghosts, the more research I do into the phenomenon, the more convinced I am that an additional supernatural element is at work. Theater owners, managers and employees have often alluded to the idea that their "house" (as insiders call the auditorium of a theater) is not only haunted but also has what could almost be called a life of its own. For example, one theater manager told me that he could "feel a cold breath emanating from the theater itself," while another indicated that her theater "has a soul."

After reading the following stories, you may find yourself agreeing.

Eccentric Entity

David Belasco was an accomplished American theatrical producer in the early days of the 20th century. He was the first to recognize and promote the money-making potential of "America's Sweetheart," Mary Pickford. Many other actresses—those with perhaps lesser talents—he merely exploited and tossed aside.

Belasco was an eccentric's eccentric. He decorated both his home and his office in the style of a monastery and dressed in a monk's habit. As previously implied, this affectation did not in any way indicate that he led a life of celibacy. His occasionally manipulative and unorthodox methods of selecting actresses for his plays were infamous throughout the world of the stage. Many fledgling young chorus girls reported that their careers advanced more rapidly after they accepted Belasco's invitation to take the private elevator up to the inner sanctum atop the Belasco Theater at 337 South Main Street in Los Angeles for the purpose of a one-on-one "audition."

History has since shown Belasco's self-serving behavior to be astonishingly persistent. Even after his death in 1931, that same elevator could be heard starting up in the evenings around 11:00. Those who were in the theater at that hour often heard the cables strain as the lift was propelled from the stage area straight up to Belasco's rooms. This might have been just a routine electrical malfunction, except that the cables had long since rusted, deteriorated and broken—snapped completely in two—and were totally incapable of elevating *anything*.

In spite of this physical impossibility, party sounds frequently followed the phantom ascent to the empty upper floor. Doors were heard opening and closing, followed by the sounds of footfalls, laughter and singing. Also, the heavy stage curtain would occasionally rise, hover dramatically for a moment, and then slowly lower again when no one was anywhere near the curtain's pulleys.

In life, Belasco had been thoroughly accepting of life "beyond the veil." In fact, his mother had appeared to him at the exact moment of her death. Belasco was a strong and flamboyant personality, so it's really not much of a surprise that his spirit was also strong—strong enough that, in addition to the ghostly elevator rides and parties, his apparition was frequently seen sitting in his box seat, watching performances on the stage. If the ghost observed all of the goings-on in the theater as the years went by, he could not have been pleased; his once elegant palace of theatrical arts did not age well. By the 1960s, the Belasco Theater had become known as the Follies Theater and had been reduced to hosting second-class strip shows. Even so, its status as a haunted theater not only remained, but actually increased after an unhappy young stripper hanged herself in the building.

The apparition of the dead stripper was so solid that those seeing her initially assumed she was a flesh and blood person, even though she was usually seen in the wee hours of the morning, long after the theater building had been locked. Whenever anyone approached her, she simply vanished. Many theater employees reported seeing the showgirl's ghost; her slim build, auburn hair, yellow sweater and brown skirt made her easily recognizable.

Staff credited this entity with a fair number of the ghostly hijinx around the theater—such as when the ropes used for raising and lowering backdrop scenery were seen moving erratically, even though no one was near them. Those movements were so powerful that the ropes could not be held still, yet when a worker called out a command to stop, those same ropes immediately steadied themselves. Witnesses reason that since the stripper chose to hang herself, the sad woman's specter may still have a penchant for rope.

Either this same ghost also appeared in her "working clothes" or the theater had yet another spirit. A prize-fighter named Johnnie Lattimore, who worked at the Belasco to keep himself afloat financially between bouts, often saw a ghost wearing only a white negligee. He would chase after her until the image disappeared into thin air. Lattimore also heard the woman's soft footsteps in the otherwise empty theater.

The once-grand, decrepit theater was eventually torn down. While passers-by still occasionally see the stripper's ghost, Belasco himself seems to have gone on to his final resting place.

A Kiss from Beyond

Dana Andersen fondly recalls his experiences at the old Mayfield Theater in Santa Monica. It was the late 1980s, and the up and coming comedian-actor was playing in the Second City Revue. One night, he had a bit of a romantic encounter with a ghost, which he described this way:

"The comedians were on stage, but other members of the cast had accessibility to observe what was happening on the stage by watching through doors and breaks in the curtains. We frequently peeked through those curtains or doors to follow the show," Dana began. He went on to acknowledge that, on one particular evening when he was covertly watching the show, he began to experience a strong sense that he was not alone.

"I felt someone come up behind me to share my 'knothole,'" Dana said. At first, he thought nothing of it—after all, it was normal procedure for the actors to crowd together at the few available spaces. "I was so comfortable with the presence that, thinking it was one of my colleagues, I started talking to it about what was happening on stage. Moments later I turned around to see who had joined me and realized there was no one with me. At least not anyone I could see."

The incident intrigued Dana and he never forgot it. He'd long suspected that the theater had a ghost. That's why, when he found himself in the green room behind the backstage area a year later, watching three other actors on stage via a video camera and television set, he was not too surprised to hear a very loud peal of giggling, high-pitched laughter. "It was a woman's laugh," he explained. "A mischievous giggle. Everyone heard it."

Another night, Dana was behind the stage and once again peering through the curtains when he had his third and most dramatic encounter with the presence in the theater.

"I was pressing my nose right up to the wall at the edge of the curtain, watching what was going on in the show, when I felt a big kiss—smack, right on the lips!"

That incident tweaked Dana Andersen's curiosity to a point where he felt he *had* to start making inquiries.

"The theater manager told me that if you sat in the darkened, empty theater with all the lights off and listened very closely, you could almost make out that someone was on stage. He was right. A group of us tried it. It was as though there was someone there but not quite there—perhaps on a parallel plane."

Explaining the results of his investigations, Dana continued: "The theater was about 100 years old. Many years ago, a diva was scheduled to sing an aria there but she died in a house fire before she was able to perform. It's generally accepted that she is the ghost."

That history certainly fits well with Dana's experiences—being joined by another curious soul, hearing the feminine laughter, and especially receiving the ghostly kiss.

Time for a Haunting

The Gray Lady who haunted the Primrose Theater in Los Angeles was known well enough to warrant a mention in the newspaper when the old place was finally torn down. Her ghostly presence was described as "hover[ing] near an old clock at the top of the foyer stairs." Over the years, many theater patrons had reported seeing her manifestation. She never bothered anyone. As a matter of fact, those who saw her were convinced that the image was incapable of connection with this realm.

An investigation into the history of both the apparition and the theater explains not only the identity of the ghost, but also the reason she haunted her particular spot. To begin that investigation, we must travel back in time to 1897, when Rosemary Primrose Adelaide Gibson Myers took over control of a playhouse that had already been in her family for two generations. To do this, the young woman had to move west and leave her successful career on New York's vaudeville stages, where she'd been known simply as "Miss Gibson."

Although she may have missed the excitement of performing, Rosemary certainly made the right decision from a financial standpoint. The late 1800s were a time of enormous economic growth. California was booming, and the industry that would eventually become known as show business was rapidly developing into a profitable venture for anyone fortunate enough to have a stake in it. Rosemary's "stake" in the family firm became much more than just financial; her entire life revolved around the Primrose Theater. She even lived in the building.

From the outside, the Primrose was somewhat nondescript and was once described as "looking more like a large candy shop than a theater." The interior was also apparently unusual, but in the more positive sense of having been decorated with great care and attention. For years, a unique clock was a focal point of the décor. The handsome timepiece had been custom made of lemonwood and rosewood at the request of Rosemary's grandfather, the original owner of the theater. Each night before retiring to her suite, Rosemary would stop at the top of the staircase where the clock stood. Only after carefully winding the precious family heirloom would she proceed to bed.

As the years went by, Rosemary decided that she'd soon be ready to pass the responsibility for the business on to a younger family member. She chose her granddaughter, Shirlee-Ann, to be her beneficiary. The choice was unsurprising because Rosemary had raised the girl. Even so, Rosemary knew that the young woman was spoiled and headstrong. In an effort to help the young woman mature and to teach her the theater business, Rosemary arranged for Shirlee-Ann to travel to New York City.

Unfortunately, as soon as the ungrateful girl arrived in the exciting eastern city, she met a ne'er-do-well actor named Leonard Banks. Rather than attending to the acquisition of theater management skills, Shirlee-Ann devoted her time in New York to developing her relationship with Banks. Much to her disappointment, she could not convince her beloved to marry her no matter how hard she worked at being his ideal mate.

When Rosemary caught wind of what was happening, she summoned the rebellious girl home. The older woman was relieved to hear that her silly granddaughter had not married the questionable man with whom she'd been cavorting. Despite her relief, Rosemary informed Shirlee-Ann that, because the young woman had chosen to ignore the training that had been offered to her, she would no longer be the recipient of the theater. Another heir would become the new owner. All Rosemary wanted from Shirlee-Ann now was the assurance that the young woman would take care of the magnificent clock that had belonged to her own grand-father, Shirlee-Ann's great-great-grandfather.

Shirlee-Ann, furious at having been cut out of the will and at being called away from her New York lover, refused to oblige her grandmother's one simple request. Although she assured Rosemary that she was taking good care of the clock, it seemed that the younger woman viewed the timepiece as a symbolic extension of her grandmother. For this reason, Shirlee-Ann made a point *not* to wind the clock. It seemed to her that in this way she had at least a small amount of figurative power over her grand-mother. Even if Shirlee-Ann could not will her domineering benefactor to die, she could, by not winding the clock, deprive her grandmother's prized possession of life.

After studiously ignoring the clock for a few days, the symbol-ism became more and more real to Shirlee-Ann. She began to wonder what it would take to actually deprive her grandmother of life. When her mind fled off in that direction, she couldn't help but think of her dear Leonard's musings about slipping "some-thing in the old bag's medicine." Such inclinations should not have been too surprising; after all, Banks had a potentially *very* wealthy girlfriend. But first Shirlee-Ann would have to ensure that it was she, and not another, who was named as the beneficiary in Rosemary's will.

Toward that end, Shirlee-Ann began to direct all of her charm at her grandmother. The old woman was soon swayed and changed her will to once again name her devious granddaughter as the sole heir. As soon as that task had been accomplished, Shirlee-Ann knew she'd have to act quickly—there was no guar-antee that Rosemary wouldn't change her mind, and her will, again. Wasting no time, the wily girl delivered a lethal cocktail to her grandmother. To ensure that Rosemary swallowed every deadly drop, Shirlee-Ann sat with her unsuspecting grandmother while the entire drink was consumed. The poor poisoned woman's dying words assured her selfish granddaughter that the will was "in a safe place." Unfortunately, the poison took effect before Shirlee-Ann could learn exactly where that "safe place" might be.

The next morning Shirlee-Ann sent an urgent telegram to Leonard Banks. "Come at once," it read. Next, while playing the role of the grieving granddaughter, she contacted the authorities and had Rosemary's body removed from the suite above the theater. Once that had been attended to, Shirlee-Ann paid a visit to the office of her grandmother's lawyer.

"My grandmother told me that her new will named me as the sole owner of the Primrose Theater," she stated.

"That's correct," the lawyer replied. "She did make the change of beneficiary from your cousin back to you just yesterday—but I don't have a copy of the latest version of her will here. You'll have to find her personal copy and bring it to me."

Frantic, Shirlee-Ann rushed back to her aunt's suite at the theater. The old woman had been virtually bedridden for weeks, so the new will *had* to be hidden somewhere in Rosemary's suite of rooms on the upper floor. Shirlee-Ann tore her grandmother's bedroom apart in a vain attempt to locate the document. Despite her determination and thoroughness, the increasingly agitated young woman was not rewarded. Several days later, when Leonard arrived, they widened the fruitless search to include the other rooms in the upstairs suite and then the entire theater.

As the despicable pair made their way down the stairs, Shirlee-Ann noticed something quite remarkable: The hands on the clock that her grandmother loved so dearly had come to rest at 10:00—the exact time the murdered woman passed away. This coincidence frightened the young woman so much that for the very first time—she opened the door to the timekeeping mechanism, wound the spring, and gave the pendulum a bit of a push. Shirlee-Ann was relieved to see the clock instantly spring to life. But those feelings of relief were short-lived; after just a few beats, the clock's movement abruptly ceased. Shirlee-Ann repeated her actions, but again the pendulum swung only a few times before coming to rest.

Leonard Banks had been impatiently watching what he thought was a display of ineptitude. He roughly shoved the would-be heiress aside and grabbed the clock with both hands, intending to give it a shake. As he did, the clock slid off its pedestal and fell toward his screaming fiancée. The weight of the massive time-piece, combined with Shirlee-Ann's shock, was enough to forcefully propel the young woman backwards down the stairs.

As Leonard and various members of the theater staff who had heard the commotion hurried to Shirlee-Ann's side, they saw immediately that she was dead. Beside her outstretched hand lay an envelope containing Rosemary Primrose Adelaide Gibson Myers's last will and testament. Shirlee-Ann's grandmother had done just as she'd said she would—she had willed everything to her granddaughter. If only Shirlee-Ann had taken care of her grandmother's beloved clock as she'd promised to do, she would have found the will quite easily. It had been hidden for safekeeping in the works of the grand old timepiece.

In a final irony, Leonard Banks discovered that if he had married Shirlee-Ann, rather than stubbornly refusing to do so, he would have had a legitimate claim to the generous estate. As it was, justice was served and the scheming man was left empty-handed.

Knowing the story behind the haunting at the Primrose Theater doesn't leave much doubt as to why the Gray Lady was frequently seen hovering near a certain old clock at the top of the foyer steps.

The Phantom Prom Queen

With all the ghostly activity at the Ventura Theatre, on South Chestnut Street in Ventura, California, it would be hard for anyone to deny that the place is haunted. Perhaps this is why the management and staff not only acknowledge that their grand old theater has a little extra "spirit," but they're also very obliging about telling the stories connected with Chester and Isabel, their resident ghosts.

Those two entities are very different from one another. Isabel is the spirit of a teenage girl. Amateur ghost hunter and former theater employee Nathan Beavers explains that the young woman was "killed when she was on stage being crowned as Prom Queen. A piece of lighting equipment dropped [from overhead] and decapitated her."

Judging by her patterns as a ghost, Isabel must have died so suddenly that she hasn't yet realized that she's no longer alive. Or her spirit may just be content to eternally relive the happy first hours of what became a tragic night.

"You can see her walking at stage right once in a while," Nathan said. "She walks toward the stage and down the dance floor. She'll come up and stand next to you. She doesn't try to harm you. She's wearing a really elegant dress, either 'whitish' in color or an extremely light pink."

Nathan's friend and former colleague, Dustin Wagner, has also been a witness to Isabel's ethereal presence. "It's kind of weird," he said. "She's on stage, usually. To me, Isabel seemed more like a shadow than a real girl."

Quite appropriately, Dustin has most often seen this shadow

when the haunted area is illuminated only by a piece of lighting equipment known as a "ghost light." He described the device this way: "It's a halogen light. It's just a freestanding bulb, a ball on a stick. It's really just to light the way. It's called a ghost light because, if it's placed in the dark, all you see is one bulb—or orb—levitating on a stick. That throws a strange light, and I've noticed human shadows, different amounts of moving shadows."

Could it be, I wondered, that there was someone standing near the ghost light to create such an outline? No, Dustin assured me—these sightings occurred when no human being was nearby.

Dustin and Nathan are not the only employees to become aware of Isabel's presence. Phil, the bartender at the Ventura, describes some of his encounters with the ghost on a Website he has created. On the evening of Saturday, April 25, 1998, Phil postponed an attempt to contact Isabel directly because a high school prom was scheduled to be held in the theater at that time. Isabel apparently wanted to attend the dance, not the séance. Phil respectfully obliged, and a few moments later another member of the staff watched in awe as the mysterious image of a girl meeting Isabel's description walked onto the dance floor.

Chester is a ghost of an entirely different nature. His background is not as well known as Isabel's. We do know that he worked—and was killed—at the theater 50 or more years ago. Although his death was officially declared to have been an accident, many people now believe that Chester was murdered.

"Chester was installing or fixing the chandelier," Nathan told me. "I figure someone pulled the ladder out from under him, because why else would his spirit stay in the theater? There has to be a reason why he's so angry. He's almost a poltergeist kind of ghost. Keys disappear, and sometimes the chairs get moved and thrown. It's *always* cold when he's there."

Dustin had an amazing experience with what he assumes was Chester's ghost. "We had a show just a while back—on February 7, 2000," he began. "I moved the barricade that we use at punk shows to keep the kids off the stage and keep the band safe because this show didn't require it."

However, Dustin did leave the portable steps leading to the stage in place. These he described as "huge wooden blocks—they're about 250 pounds each, and they butt right up against the stage so you can walk right up. I can barely budge one of these things. I can pick it up by a side and I can slide it and drag it, but that's all."

In an effort to overcome some of the limitations of a telephone interview, Dustin kindly explained that he is "not a little guy—I weigh 230 pounds."

The show went on and all went well. The next day, the staff had to once again rearrange the set-up to prepare for a performance by the punk band. This meant removing the steps to the stage and putting the barrier back in place. When the workers went to the spot where the barricade was stored, they were almost unable to believe their eyes. There, behind the stored barricade, was one of the enormous wooden steps.

In addition to the unimaginable logistics involved in moving the massive wooden block to that awkward location, Dustin knew for certain that absolutely no one had been in the theater. He'd been the last one to leave after the performance and, just before he locked up, he had observed that *all* of the steps were right where they should have been—leading up to the stage.

What Dustin and two other workers found the next time they entered the theater spooked them all. "One of those giant stair blocks had been thrown behind the barricade," he said. "Not stacked like stairs or anything—just casually tossed, like it was as light as a rag doll. I totally think it was Chester."

Having been given a demonstration of the ghost's abilities, Dustin must have been extremely uncomfortable with the realization that "Chester's ghost doesn't like me. I get this feeling like I shouldn't be alone in certain places," he admitted. "Lately I've been doing repair work on the place. Ever since I've started doing that kind of thing, all of a sudden it's like I've been targeted."

While he was trying to clean one of the chandeliers in the building, Dustin had a distressing experience. "I was up on this old rickety ladder and reaching out to change a light bulb, but it kept getting farther and farther away," he said. "I kept stretching and reaching, and then I thought, 'Wait a second—I should have grabbed it by now!' But whenever I went to reach for the bulb, it visibly moved away from my hand. I'm thinking this is just like a scene from a classic horror movie and I'm going to fall and decapitate myself on the bars of the chandelier. So I thought, 'I'm going to outsmart this guy.' I crawled up higher, grabbed the chain of the chandelier, and pulled the whole fixture toward me."

Having won that particular battle with the angry phantom, Dustin hastily changed the bulb that had required his attention before gratefully climbing down the ladder to the safety of the floor below.

On another occasion, Dustin was waiting for other workers to join him at a remote corner of the theater. "When I saw a light click on and tan pants and black shoes—like the kind I usually wear—going up a ladder, I thought, 'Okay, someone's already up there,'" he said. "So I started to follow, but I noticed right away that the door to go up to the roof wasn't open! When I lookedinside the door, no one was in there. I called out 'hello' and no one answered, so I said, 'Screw this—I'm not going in.' I felt like Chester wanted to get me alone."

Dustin and Nathan were together the time that Dustin "chased a cold spot. I ended up getting thrown on the ground. It happened in the bar in the theater. I think that was Chester, too."

Something about the old theater must have created an inviting home for wandering spirits because, in addition to Chester and Isabel, Nathan Beavers described "faces you can see that pop out of the darkness—and then you turn on the lights and there's no one there."

The next time the theater was active it was being used to host a "goth club" get-together. ("Goths" are described by sociologist Dr. Barrie Robinson as being "an offshoot of the punk movement, identified mainly for their fascination with the supernatural, mysticism, and for some, the occult; in particular, a fascination for vampires and the undead. [People adhering to this subculture] have a penchant for black clothes, white makeup on their faces, black lipstick and black fingernails, thereby evoking images of the walking undead and a general sense of nihilism/despair.") Ventura Theatre employees decorated the place accordingly, even including a dummy of a ghostly angel with a skeleton face. As Dustin puts it, "The goths like that kind of stuff, so we were just trying to make them happy."

That thoughtfulness nearly had a disastrous outcome. "We hung the dummy on a rope from the front of the stage and it just swung around. It would swing around for no reason. At one point it started to fall, to burn through like someone was burning the rope, but there was nothing—no heat on the rope whatsoever. Nothing and no one was up there in a position to burn it like that."

It is not clear what caused that anomaly. Perhaps Chester did not approve of the decorations. What *is* clear is that the Ventura Theatre is a very unusual place employing some extraordinary people work—and hosting at least two very persuasive ghosts.

Harmlessly Haunted

Part of the building that houses a San Jose-area theater dates back to the mid-1800s, when it was built for a general of the Union Army. Even the "new" section has stood for 50 years. This long history has allowed more than sufficient time for the place to become haunted—which it most certainly is.

The ghost of a man in a Civil War uniform probably dates back to the days when the building was used to hold Confederate sympathizers. Without warning, the eerie image has been known to appear at an upstairs window. He seems to be grasping at his chest with one hand while apparently reaching out for help with the other. Moments later, he vanishes—either by walking through a wall or by becoming less and less distinct until he is no longer visible.

A more modern ghost seems to be that of a woman. Although she has never been seen, she's certainly been heard by many people as her high-heeled shoes tap a path across the floor of an area that is invariably known to be vacant at the time. We do not know which of the entities haunting the historic building is responsible for turning on strobe lights that were unplugged at the time they began to flash!

The ghosts are certainly not malicious. Of course, they do create the inevitable cold spots throughout the place and that slightly disconcerting feeling for the staff that they are being watched—even when they can plainly see that there is no one in the room with them. The presences also like to draw attention to themselves, oftentimes by playing their own music. They have also demonstrated a playful sense of humor by causing draft beer to come out of one spigot when a staff member had opened a *different* tap.

It's Helen Here

While researching and compiling ghost stories, I received the following story in the form of a wonderful letter from Donald C. Hepner on behalf of John and Lynne Schlenker, the owners and producers of The Great American Melodrama and Vaudeville in Oceano. The missive is dated January 21, 1998.

"The Great American Melodrama has been in existence for 23 years. The brief history is that the theater was begun in an abandoned drugstore in Oceano. The drugstore was abandoned by the owner after his wife's unfortunate and untimely death. The lady, Helen, died at the drugstore. The owners had a 'day room' in the back of the store and they used this room for lunch, to watch television, or to rest. One afternoon, Helen retired to this room to lie down, since she had a stomach ache. She never

The tech crew at the Great American Melodrama and Vaudeville in Oceano believes their theater is home to a playful phantom named Helen.

awakened. In despair, Joshua Allen, Helen's husband, closed the doors and abandoned the drugstore altogether.

"From what we have learned about Helen, she was a 'childlike' 40-year-old when she died. Helen had a wonderful sense of humor and enjoyed life very much. It is this ghost or spirit that haunts The Great American Melodrama. Obvious examples of Helen's 'spiritness' to us at the theater come in the forms of tools and props that seemingly disappear and then reappear at different locations and at different times.

"When we get into 'tech week'—and 'tech week' turns into 'tech from hell week'—Helen gets annoyed with us and even more 'hell' breaks out from 'Hell-en.' Apart from that, Helen is a sweet and gentle spirit.

"Perhaps all of the events we attribute to Helen could be logically explained by outsiders, but we here at the Melodrama, we who live and work with Helen, know Helen is our 'ghostly sprite.' We love her! It is also easier to blame a ghost for the unexplainable, especially since superstitions run rampant in the theater trade."

Donald closes his letter with the charming salutation, "Spiritually yours."

Although we have no indication that Helen has left her home in the drugstore-cum-theater, a more recent letter advises, "No new 'Helen' sightings to report."

Haunted Sacramento Theaters

The heart of Sacramento is a well-haunted area. According to my research, it has been so for a very long time. In the 1930s, a ghostly anecdote dating from the mid-1800s was finally made public. It was only then that the public learned that the Turner Waxwork Theater, an attraction which only existed until 1885, had been haunted by a possessed mannequin.

After observing frightening paranormal signs, such as inanimate figurines that moved by themselves, the staff was horrified to discover upon opening the building one morning that one of the figures had been not only moved, but totally destroyed. The remains of the statue lay by the doorway in a heap. Its fingers had been hideously disfigured. When the staff locked the building the evening before, all was as it should have been. In the morning, despite the damage to the figure, there were no signs that anyone had broken into the place.

In an early and rather ghoulish version of recycling efficiency, the wax in the hideously damaged figure was melted down and made into another statue. There was never any further ghostly activity at the Turner Waxwork Theater.

The Sacramento Theatre Company on H Street is one seriously haunted building. The ghost of the McClatchy Mainstage has been seen numerous times over the years by employees, actors and even patrons. His presence is so accepted by those associated with the theater that they have named him. "Pinky," as the ghost is affectionately known, has always been thought of as a protective spirit; after an incident in 1990, at least three employees are convinced that Pinky is the theater's guardian.

The three were rigging stage lighting. One man was standing on the stage itself while two others worked high above him when, in the same instant, all three felt the temperature in the area drop markedly. They'd worked around the haunted theater long enough to know that the sudden blast of cold was a sure sign that the ghost was present. Moments later, the man who was standing below the others was overcome by a premonition of great impending danger. He called out for his co-workers to stop what they were doing and come down from the scaffolding immediately. Upon hearing the urgent tone of their colleague's voice, the two obeyed without question. Seconds later, a light bar crashed down onto the stage. If the two men had still been up at the level of those lights, they would've been badly injured or even killed. To this day, those theater technicians are grateful to Pinky for possibly having saved their lives.

Psychics and clairvoyants who've toured the Sacramento Theatre have found that Pinky has other ghosts to keep him company in his eternity. People have heard the sounds of a woman walking in high-heeled shoes when there was no one visible in the room. These sounds have even been recorded on audio tapes. Other inexplicable irregularities have shown up in photographs— tubes, orbs and irregularly shaped streaks of light have all appeared in otherwise ordinary pictures of the playhouse. Inevitably, there was no such illumination in the area at the time the anomalous shots were taken.

A psychic named Robin Street described a male ghost who inhabits the Costume Department. From her description and the theater's records, it was discerned that this spirit was a former wardrobe supervisor. The man had been utterly devoted to his job and returned after death to watch over the area. Street's description of the phantom—a middle-aged man with light colored eyes who wears glasses and is about five feet, eight inches tall—matched the deceased's description precisely, even though the psychic had no prior knowledge of the man.

With dedicated staff members who continue to look out for the theater even in death, the Sacramento Theatre Company is almost certain to have a long, successful, haunted future.

Melodramatic Spirit

The history of the theater known as the Moorpark Melodrama dates back to 1928, when it was built as a silent movie house. It was not long before the Melodrama became "the only talking movie theater in the east end of Ventura County." According to the current owner, from that time until the "mid-1950s, the Melodrama was the social focal point for the entire community." Parts of the building have served a multitude of functions. The snack bar was for a time the town's malt shop. A dentist once spent his days in a box office that had been renovated to suit his purposes. A library, a hairdressing salon, and even a school were temporarily housed in the building.

When contacted about the possibility of ghosts inhabiting the old place, Linda Bredemann, current owner of the Moorpark Melodrama, had a very different take on the concept of a haunted theater. While acknowledging that actors who've worked in the theater have assured her that there are at least two ghosts in residence—a male and a female—Linda believes that "the theater itself has a soul, and that is a different thing."

Linda went on to explain, "I know when the theater's feeling sad and I know when it's not. Some people would interpret that as a ghost, but to me it's just the spirit of the theater. You can tell when the theater is happy about what's happening in it and when it's not. Right now, she's feeling very sad. I call her a female. Now when you go in there you can feel the difference in the theater. It's probably just because there's no laughter in there any more and you can feel that she's sad. That's why I've tried for the last three years to keep her going."

And Linda is apparently not the only one able to read the theater's moods—others have felt them, too. "She [the theater] doesn't like men," the forthright owner acknowledged. Linda even implied that the theater itself might have had a hand in "choosing" her as its owner. "I've talked to the former owner," she says. "We have a *lot* in common and we're both exactly four feet, ten inches tall."

Coincidence? Possibly—but while considering Linda Bredemann's first-hand experience, it's tough to dismiss her theory out of hand. Whether it's the presence of ghosts that her actors claim are there, or the palpable soul of the theater that Linda herself senses, there's something very special in at least one of Moorpark's theaters.

Ghostly Critic

Alfred, the ghost at the Conejo Valley Playhouse in Thousand Oaks, is nothing if not loyal. This community theater had its humble beginnings in an old barn—probably, as it turns out, a haunted barn. Jean Murray, who has been associated with the theater for some time, indicated that most people feel Alfred's spirit was in the barn when they took it over.

The ghost must have been lonely in his hereafter, because he soon became an integral part of the show. If Alfred didn't like a particular production, the cast knew they would be in for a noisy review from beyond. Footsteps would be heard clomping up and down the aisle, props would mysteriously move about, and some

A ghost named Alfred always lets the cast and crew at the Conejo Players Theatre in Thousand Oaks know how he feels about a particular performance.

of the actors' personal items would occasionally go missing. Alfred would eventually return whatever he had taken, but he always kept the articles long enough to be a nuisance to the actor. This meant that there was no way the living could miss Alfred's displeasure with a performance.

Despite ghostly interference—or possibly *because* of the direction it provided—the theater company grew and prospered. When the troupe moved to larger premises, many people wondered whether they might be leaving Alfred behind. Not so, according to Jean Murray. "He hangs around," she explained. "He rattles doors and scares newcomers. If he likes the show, he's pretty good. But if he doesn't like a show, the coffee pot will not come on or something like that."

Actors often lament that everyone in the world is a critic. At the Conejo Valley Playhouse, that axiom must be amended to include one "out of this world" critic.

Phantom of the Opera House

When I called the Woodland Opera House to find out more about their ghost, I was immediately told, "You need to talk to Nadine." What great advice that turned out to be! Not only was Nadine Salonites extremely knowledgeable about the theater's history, she was delightfully personable and outgoing. Better still, even after accompanying and observing "ghost hunters" who'd come into the theater to investigate—and having had a few rather mysterious experiences herself—she was still guardedly skeptical. In short, Nadine was an ideal person to interview about a haunted theater.

My initial source for this story had included a reference to "a shy ghost" whose "presence is presaged by the odor of cigar smoke." Nadine laid that rumor to rest in her opening sentence: "I've been around the Opera House since 1971, and I really can't imagine where that one came from."

For just a moment, I was disappointed—certain that my promising lead had fizzled to a non-story. Not so; Nadine immediately added, "*We do* have a situation here."

Given the long and varied history of the Woodland Opera House, it's not much wonder that the venerable institution is home to a ghost. "This is not the first Opera House [on the site]," Nadine explained. "The first one was built in 1885 and burned down in 1892. We're in a valley [roughly 30 miles northwest of Sacramento] that is prone to very strong north winds, particularly in June and July. There was one very, very forceful north wind in the summer of 1892 and somebody dropped a cigarette on some

Renovated and reopened to the public in 1971, the historic Woodland Opera House is haunted by a phantom firefighter who perished while fighting a blaze at the theater in 1892.

dry grass in the lot behind the Opera House. That started on fire, and the fire jumped over to the Opera House. One of the Woodland firemen was trying to get some hoses out when the back wall fell on him and killed him." The fire continued to rage and consumed much of downtown Woodland before its destructive force was finally tamed. It is generally accepted that the spirit haunting the Opera House is that of the doomed fireman.

According to Nadine, rumors of the haunting have attracted many paranormal researchers to the theater. "We've had several of them come to check out the Opera House," she confirmed. "They have all arrived with some kind of equipment, some more sophisticated than others. One had cameras that are supposed to show hidden things, and I actually saw things [through those cameras] that you don't see with a naked eye. It was kind of fun. I'm not totally sold on it, I must say. I'm a bit skeptical, but it was fun."

On another occasion, a group of people interested in developing their psychic powers toured the building. "They began at the very tip-top of the Opera House and went looking and looking, trying to feel unusual things," Nadine said. "They finally ended up in the basement. The gist of it is that whenever anyone finds anything out of the ordinary, all of them find the activity in the basement."

One group of researchers brought equipment that was designed to detect electrical activity and hauled it down to the basement area. "Well, you know, there's a *lot* of electrical equipment down in the basement," Nadine explained. Therefore, she was not surprised when the researchers' apparatus gave a high reading. She was surprised, however, when the investigators walked over to the side of the basement where the electrical equipment was actually located—and the audible readings on their instruments stopped all at once. "Then they'd come back over to the other side," Nadine continued. "They'd move away from the electrical equipment, and the noise would get much, much louder."

This finding fits well with the theory that the ghost is that of the firefighter killed so long ago, because this is the area where his body would have landed after the wall collapsed on him. Also, at that very spot, Nadine herself had an accident.

"I was doing musical direction," she said. "The show was *Gerry's Girls*, which has a cast of six women singers. I was downstairs with the performers afterwards. When I started to go upstairs, my foot just kind of caught on a rug we have on the floor down there, and I just took a splat, face down."

Fortunately, Nadine wasn't seriously hurt in the fall, but she still wonders what might have caused the accident, because it was in the very spot where she fell that all the paranormal investigators found ghostly activity.

Another incident that occurred "in that same general area" could have been extremely serious if the timing had been just a little different. "Before the theater was restored, I did a lot of opening and closing of the building," Nadine explained. "We had wine and cheese parties where we'd just invite people from town. We'd invite 25 or 30 at a time, just to get them inside the facility to see it. Because the Opera House had been closed from 1913 to 1971, most folks had seen the outside but had never been inside. We wanted to get people excited about it, so we scooped out as much of the dirt as we could and shored up places where [the structure] was sagging badly. It was after one of those wine and cheese functions that I went to the basement, turned out the lights, and came upstairs. I was ready to go out when I heard this big crash in the back of the building. Right there in the stairwell area where I had been just a short while before, and where quite a few people had been going up and down the steps earlier in the day, a huge plank fell from high up above—right into the stairwell."

Even though she maintains that she's still somewhat skeptical, Nadine does concede that "if you start putting little things together, they start making sense." In addition to the incidents she experienced and related to me, "a few other people have had experiences"—such as the Opera House secretary who watched in amazement as ghost lights danced about the interior of the otherwise darkened auditorium.

Talking about the "situation" in her beloved Opera House seemed to reinforce Nadine's acceptance of the ghost's existence because, in conclusion, she asserted, "He's not harmful. The interesting thing is that [the firefighter] had an old Victorian cottage here in Woodland. People are living in there now, and some say that they have some very interesting things happening. Maybe he goes back and forth."

Perhaps the phantom of this particular Opera House is more real to Nadine than even she knows.

Chapter 8

SPIRIT SNIPPETS

Although it is always gratifying to find an authentic ghost story that is completely intact, we must often settle for mere fragments of tales.
Some of the following stories are examples of instances where the details of a haunting have been lost to history.

Readers occasionally tell me that they find this lack of completeness frustrating, but I've come to appreciate these fragments for their longevity alone.
A few of the following anecdotes have been passed along from person to person so many times that they have virtually become contemporary legends.
Some of the accounts in this section are not even truly ghost stories. They are, however, fascinating accounts of paranormal incidents.

How Could They Know?

On June 4, 1968, the morning service at a church in Los Angeles was interrupted by an elderly woman. In hysterics, she threw herself across the altar. Several women from the congregation approached her, offered comfort, and led the crying woman away.

When she had calmed down sufficiently to speak, the elderly woman confided the reason that she was upset. "Yesterday I touched the hand of Bobby Kennedy," she sobbed. "Bobby will emerge victorious ... but that victory will be short-lived. When I touched his hand, I felt the presence of death."

Two days later Robert F. Kennedy was dead.

California-based events that appear to touch on the paranormal also surround the assassination of President John F. Kennedy on November 22, 1963. At 10:10 on that tragic morning, the telephone company in Oxnard, 50 miles north of Los Angeles, received what they initially thought was a prank call. The voice that spoke seemed to belong to a distraught woman. She said simply, "The president is going to be killed." Just 20 minutes later, the infamous shots rang out in Dallas, Texas.

Long Distance Call

In January 1934, a woman in the eastern United States was awakened by a phone call. Her name was Mrs. Gandy, and she had a son named Arne who was living on the west coast in the San Francisco area. She did not recognize the voice on the line, nor did she understand the message that it gave her. "The kid is here … forgive him … what I said about him is all true … he is a fine kid."

Then, for a while, there seemed to be more than one voice speaking and Mrs. Gandy could also make out people laughing. "I am helpless," one voice uttered. "He's in bad shape—he's on his way home," another declared.

At that point, the line went dead. Mrs. Gandy contacted a telephone operator, who told her that the call had originated in San Francisco. Realizing that the information she'd overheard could pertain to her son and his well-being, she called the San Francisco Police Department. The next day, authorities found Arne Gandy's body in the bay and determined that he had drowned at least two days earlier.

With reasonable justification, the deceased man's mother believes that she received word of her son's death via a phone call from beyond.

Time Travelers

Some students of the paranormal maintain that ghost sightings are actually slips in time—shifts in perception that allow us to temporarily glimpse either backward or forward in time. These phenomena are referred to as either retrocognition (seeing into the past) or precognition (seeing into the future). A very famous case of retrocognition took place during the summer of 1901, when two professors from England were visiting a formal garden in Versailles, France. As they strolled through the peaceful setting, the two woman suddenly and inexplicably became disoriented. They saw their surroundings in a strange, dream-like fashion and observed, in a detached way, people dressed in a style from two centuries before their era milling about a kiosk and a small bridge-like structure. As quickly and spontaneously as their shared hallucination had begun, it was over. They saw that they were still in the same gardens they had seen in that earlier time, but the "bridge" and the kiosk were no longer there. Further, the people wandering near them were now quite definitely dressed in contemporary clothing.

Days later, still intrigued by their experience, the two revisited the site and repeated their retrocognitive encounter. Upon returning home to England, the pair spoke enthusiastically about the unique episode. Their stories made their colleagues curious, and some of them traveled to France—where they, too, saw and even spoke with people from an era long past.

A similar occurrence happened on August 19, 1951. Two women staying in a hotel at Dieppe in France were awakened by the sounds of shellfire, dive bombing and people screaming—in short, the sounds of an air raid. The women were experiencing auditory retrocognition—the attack they were listening to had actually taken place in 1942.

Although both of those famous examples took place in France, such incidents are certainly not confined to Europe. During the Christmas shopping rush of 1966, a teenager named Elaine (her last name is in the author's files) experienced the phenomenon while shopping at a San Francisco Woolworth's store.

Many years later, Elaine explained that she had headed to the basement of the discount department store in an effort to escape the Yuletide crowds. No sooner had she made her way to the bottom of the staircase than she realized that she was "in a strange setting," a setting that she later described as looking like a general store one might have expected to find a century or more before her time.

Elaine watched in awe as the historical scene played out in front of her eyes. A potbellied stove stood in front of the store counter; a bearded man stood behind it. He and Elaine stared at one another briefly while she blinked her eyes and shook her head. But those attempts to clear her vision did nothing to alter the sight before her. Although there were four other people in the vision—three women, presumably shoppers, and a little boy—the shopkeeper was the only one who appeared to take note of Elaine's presence.

After an undetermined length of time, the teenage girl's consciousness returned to present day and she concluded the business that had brought her into the store in the first place. Since that first incident in her teens, Elaine has experienced retrocognition on several occasions. Although she does not credit herself with being particularly sensitive in other supernatural areas, she now knows that for some reason she can periodically see into the past.

Victim's Suffering Still Evident

Arlene (whose last name is also on file with the author) was a young widow when she had an unexpected and unsettling look into history. Her experience with retrocognition occurred during an evening in June 1932, as she rode a bus from her job in Los Angeles's west end to her home in the east end.

Arlene explained that the bus route ran through a commercial section of the city just before it crossed the river. She was staring out at the passing scenery when the bus slowed to negotiate a curve around 7th Street. As it did, Arlene clearly saw a horse-drawn wagon. Although this certainly startled the woman, it didn't worry her—until an old man came into view. He was just behind the wagon and appeared to be badly hurt.

Shocked by what she saw, Arlene expected the bus driver to stop and help the obviously injured man. When he didn't, she prepared to jump up from her seat and say something. It was then she noticed that no one else in the bus appeared to be aware that they had just driven past something decidedly out of the ordinary.

Arlene worried about the incident throughout the evening and she was still concerned the next morning. Because she did not have to be at work terribly early, she decided to investigate the strange scene she had witnessed. She took the bus along the same route and got off at the stop closest to where she'd seen the bizarre images. This time there was nothing unusual to be seen. Walking slowly, Arlene came to a business office. The door stood open; she went in and called out a greeting. When a man approached the counter Arlene, somewhat hesitantly, began to speak. "I passed here yesterday evening on a bus and saw an elderly man struggling behind a horse-drawn wagon," she said. "He was obviously hurt and I've been concerned about him ever since. Do you know if he's all right?"

The man behind the counter stood in silence for a moment before replying. "You're not the first to see old John," the man said finally. "John was killed out front more than 10 years ago. They found him at his horse's feet and figured he'd been hit by a car."

Either Arlene experienced retrocognition that June evening in 1932 or John's spirit was still struggling, in vain, toward the help he had needed a decade before.

Bridges to the Other Side?

At least two bridges in California are haunted. The original Jersey Bridge over the Yuba River in north central California was replaced years ago, but the ghost who haunted the old structure can still be seen.

Her name was Juanita. On July 5, 1851, an angry mob captured the young woman. Without benefit of a formal trial, the vigilantes decided that she was to blame for the murder of one of their peers. The angry men tied a noose around the terrified woman's neck, coiled the other end of the rope around a bridge support, and hurled Juanita over the railing toward the Yuba River. Seconds later, her lifeless body hung suspended above the river.

Today, a plaque on a nearby building commemorates the short life of the woman who was illegally—and possibly unjustly—

hanged from the bridge. That recognition alone was apparently not sufficient to calm the deceased's soul; people still report seeing an apparition emerge from a shroud of fog at the southeast corner of the bridge. Witnesses are consistent in their description of the entity as a young woman, and most report feeling that she is trying to communicate with them. After a few moments, the image vaporizes as mysteriously as it appears, leaving the living to ponder the nature of their curious experience.

Hundreds of miles south, just inland from Santa Barbara at Ojai, stands another haunted bridge. The phantom of the Creek Road Bridge, who has been described as "hideous" both in appearance and smell, is thought to date back to a presumably fatal car fire in the 1950s.

Those who witnessed the tragedy reported seeing a man, his clothes ablaze, fleeing from the burning automobile. All who watched the sickening event agreed that the man could not possibly have lived—but no one ever knew for certain because neither the man nor his body was ever found. It is thought that the ghost is the revenant of the man who was killed in the fire, because the apparition haunting the bridge has badly burned skin, charred clothing and smells horribly of burning flesh.

Pastoral Scene Replays

On the hills north of Ojai, a ghostly scene occasionally reaches out across time. Those who have witnessed the amazing spectacle relate seeing the image of a shepherd tending his phantom flock. According to legend, just such a man was once murdered in that area. It is supposed that the energy that was once the man's soul has simply remained on the earthly plane, still tending to his daily business.

Forest Phantom

Near Escondido, not far from where Highways 15 and 78 intersect in San Diego County, a wonderfully appealing ghost haunts the Elfin Forest. The White Lady, as she's come to be known, has a beguiling smile for all those who see her. She has even reached out her hand and placed it comfortingly on people's shoulders. Witnesses believe she's just an uncommonly friendly person— until they realize that the woman is not walking, but hovering more than a foot above the ground. Those who continue to watch the apparition say that she passes through solid objects before vanishing mysteriously into the forest.

Dreamer Detects Body

In May of 1963, John Pflovk drowned in the Tuolumne River near his home in Modesto. Despite a thorough search, his body wasn't recovered for another three and a half months. The corpse might not have been found at all if it hadn't been for a dream. Miller Sardella was one of the officers involved in the search. During the night of August 29th, he dreamed that the drowned man's body would be found near the Don Pedro Dam Reservoir Station.

Sardella decided to check the area his dream described on the off chance that the vision had been accurate. He took two deputies with him, and the trio located the body in exactly the spot where the officer had dreamed it would be found. Perhaps the spirit of John Pflovk visited the lawman in his dream so that the search would be successful and the matter—along with the drowned man's soul—could finally be put to rest.

Spirit of Inspiration

The Bradbury Building, on South Broadway in downtown Los Angeles, dates back to 1893. It may have a nondescript exterior, but its interior and its past more than make up for the bland façade. Local legend has it that George Wyman received the plans for the extravagant structure from his brother. What makes this story of sibling cooperation especially intriguing is that Wyman's brother was long-dead when the plans were revealed; the brothers communicated by means of a Ouija board.

Mission Manifestations

The Mission San Antonio de Padua in King City and the Mission La Purisima Concepcion in Lompoc have both been preserved and now stand in startling contrast to their ultra-modern surroundings in southwestern California. They are also both haunted.

The Mission San Antonio de Padua was built in 1771. According to some, it was the scene of enigmatic happenings from its earliest days. Even two and a half centuries ago, residents reported feeling random and inexplicable cold spots throughout the property, seeing strange flickering lights that didn't seem to have a source, and sensing unseen presences.

The mission is surrounded by Fort Hunter Liggett Military Base, but the bizarre illusions have not only continued but strengthened. A phantom monk, the hood of his robes obscuring his face, is sometimes seen walking peacefully along the pathways. Seconds later, the image disappears, transported back to his own dimension in time.

Richard Senate, now a well known psychic researcher, stayed at the mission for a time in the spring of 1978. When Senate arrived at the mission, his interest lay in archeology, not ghost hunting. But an encounter in the middle of the night during his stay at the mission permanently broadened the man's scope of interest.

It was after midnight and, although he was extremely tired, Senate was unable to sleep. Thinking that a snack might help him fall asleep, he made his way outside, into the courtyard and toward the mission's kitchen. As he walked he noted a figure coming toward him. This did not surprise Senate at all, as there were many archeologists as well as monks staying in the isolated buildings at the time. But when the image drew closer to him, Senate's curiosity was piqued. The monks living in the mission tended to dress in ordinary street clothes, while this person wore a hooded robe. Stranger still, whoever the monk was, he was carrying a candle.

Then the image abruptly vanished. The figure had come within roughly 12 feet of Senate before inexplicably disappearing. There were no bushes behind which a practical joker could have hidden, no buildings he could have slipped into. As Richard Senate stood and stared in amazement, he realized that he had just seen a ghost.

The next day, Senate inquired as to who it was he had seen in the night. Senate was informed that he was certainly not the first person to encounter the image. It seems that in the early 1800s, the monks of the mission observed a routine which included rising just after midnight to pray. They carried candles to light their way. Presumably the specter that had startled the sleepless Senate had simply been a remnant from long ago.

This is not the only ghost story from the area. There is a wonderfully spooky old legend about a woman who was killed by her husband. It is said that her headless apparition can still be seen riding across the property. What makes this old tale a bit more convincing than most is that many of the witnesses to her ghostly ride have been members of the military who were stationed at the base surrounding the mission. Military police have even pursued the wraith in four-wheel drive vehicles. Despite their apparent advantages, the MPs were not able to catch the phantom—she rode her steed over a hill crest on the horizon and vanished into thin air.

Another apparition is not as solid physically, but its deliberate movements have made it easy for historians at the mission to identify. Many years ago, Father John Baptist kept to a specific routine. He would walk out to admire the fish in a nearby pond before going into the chapel to pray. Several people at Mission San Antonio de Padua have reported watching in awestruck amazement as a misty vapor follows that same route.

The soul of a little girl who, when she knew she was dying, asked to be buried on the grounds of the secluded seminary is also believed to reside on the property. Her wish was granted, and delicate flowers miraculously bloom at her gravesite even in the killing desert heat.

The Mission La Purisima Concepcion has now been incorporated into a California State Park. Rangers and other employees of the park report that, no matter how many times a day they straighten it, a particular bed in one of the mission's bedrooms will not stay neat. Staff can repeatedly tidy the room and smooth the blankets on the bed, only to return a little later and find the bedclothes in disarray—with the distinct outline of a human body impressed on it.

Park Ranger Steve Jones has even seen a misty apparition in that room. Although the image is slightly transparent, it is clear enough for Jones to make out an old, long-haired man wearing a gown and sitting on the bed.

The ranger's research indicates that the manifestation is probably the ghost of Father Mariano Payeras, who died in that bedroom in 1823. Presumably his spirit is responsible for the strange outline workers so often find on the bed.

The End